1000 TIPS AND QUIPS FOR
SPEAKERS AND TOASTMASTERS

1000 TIPS AND QUIPS FOR
FOR
SPEAKERS AND
TOASTMASTERS

By

HERBERT V. PROCHNOW

BAKER BOOK HOUSE
Grand Rapids, Michigan

ISBN: 0-8010-6895-9

Library of Congress Catalog Card Number: 62-19654

Fourth printing, September 1991

Printed in the United States of America

PREFACE

This reference book contains 1,000 quips and tips for use on many different occasions by speakers and toastmasters.

The hundreds of items include epigrams and witticisms, humorous stories, literary quotations, biographical and inspirational material, unusual facts, challenging ideas and interesting observations by distinguished persons. The book also contains in outline form some basic rules for organizing and conducting meetings.

The purpose of the book is to bring to those who speak and to those who preside at meetings a wealth of helpful material to assure the successful discharge of their responsibilities. Those who speak in public, including ministers, teachers, attorneys and other groups, and all those who preside at meetings of various kinds should find many occasions when a story, a witticism, or a pertinent illustration from the book may be of assistance in the preparation of suitable remarks.

It is hoped that the general reader may likewise find in this reference book material of interest to him from time to time.

HERBERT V. PROCHNOW

CONTENTS

CHAPTER I

TIPS FOR SPEAKERS

To conserve the time of the reader there are presented in outline form in this chapter a number of suggestions for those who wish to speak more effectively and with greater assurance.

If you speak well —

1. You make your ideas clear to others.
2. You think through the subject and organize your thoughts logically.
3. You lead others to accept your ideas.
4. You find a gratifying increase in your own confidence.

Specifically, what must you do to be a good speaker?

1. You must not agree to speak on a subject regarding which you are not qualified. Nothing takes the place of knowledge of a subject.
2. You must carefully prepare every speech you give. No speaker has the right to take the time of an audience if he is not prepared.
3. Your ideas must be logically presented so your comments are convincing. This requires organization. It may be best to outline your comments, point by point.
4. The subject should be one in which the particular audience is interested.
5. When you speak it is generally best to adhere closely to the speech as you prepared it. In digressing from your remarks as you prepared them, there is always great danger that your thoughts will ramble from your specific subject.
6. Illustrations and examples which are pertinent to your subject will help you to emphasize points you wish to make.
7. Enthusiasm is essential. However, enthusiasm is largely the result of a thorough knowledge of one's subject and thorough preparation. No one can enthuse about what he doesn't know. Moreover, he cannot have confidence when he is not fully prepared.

8. Ask how much time you are to be given and do not speak longer than the time allotted.

9. Always speak clearly and sufficiently loud so you can be easily heard everywhere in the room.

10. Do not underestimate the intelligence of any group to which you speak. Every audience to which you agree to speak deserves the most thorough preparation and the best address you can give.

When you prepare your speech there are certain procedures which may help you.

1. Most speakers will probably find it helpful to divide a speech into three major parts: the introduction, the body of the speech, and the close.

2. In the introduction you make clear the subject you propose to discuss.

3. The body is the heart of the speech. For most speakers, it is probably best to divide it into two, three or four principal points. These points should be logically and thoughtfully presented. This will require you to organize your thoughts. The body of the speech should have facts, figures and illustrations, if necessary, to emphasize the points you wish to make. As a rule it is best to give the points, one by one as the speech proceeds rather than to state them at the beginning.

4. The close or conclusion of the speech should be brief. You may wish to summarize the major points you have made. You may close with a quotation from literature or the Bible or with an unusual illustration of a great moment in history or business that brings the speech to a climax. In some speeches you may close by calling for action on a proposal you have made.

CHAPTER II

TIPS FOR TOASTMASTERS

In the first chapter there were presented in outline form a number of suggestions for those who wish to speak more effectively. In this chapter there are presented in outline form suggestions for the person who presides as the chairman or toastmaster.

We shall consider first those suggestions which relate to planning the program.

1. Make certain the subject chosen for discussion at a meeting is one that will be of genuine interest to the audience.

2. Having picked the subject, make certain that the speaker chosen is highly competent to discuss the subject and will do it well. If you handle these two points properly, you almost guarantee the success of a meeting.

3. Make certain that the speaker definitely understands the subject on which he is to speak, the date and location of the meeting and the character of the audience.

4. Make arrangements, if necessary, for meeting the speaker and also for his hotel accommodations.

5. Plan a precise time schedule for the meeting and follow it.

6. Advise the speaker of the time to be given him and make certain that he is given this time. Announcements and other activities should not interfere with the time given the speaker.

7. Obtain from the speaker biographical material you can use for publicity and for your introduction.

8. Prepare publicity for the meeting and see that the speaker gets copies of any publicity.

9. Arrange for a speaker's podium and also for a public address system, if it is needed.

10. Invite those to be at the speaker's table and arrange for them to meet the speaker on the day of the meeting. Have place cards at the table to show where each guest is to be seated.

11. Obtain the necessary information to introduce each guest properly. The guests should be introduced loudly and plainly so everyone hears each person's name. The introductions should be brief.

12. Prepare the introduction of the speaker. Remember in your introduction that the speaker is to make the speech and not the chairman.

On the day of the meeting you may wish to see that the room is in proper order with good ventilation, the public address system in good working condition, and a speaker's podium ready.

In your introduction of the speaker you may find it helpful to keep these points in mind.

1. The introduction should commend the speaker but it should not be so extravagant that the speaker cannot live up to it no matter how well he speaks.

2. The introduction should give sufficient facts about the speaker so his competence to speak on the subject is clearly established and so the members of the audience feel that they know him.

3. It is often possible to use humor effectively in the introduction.

4. Sometimes it is possible to "kid" the speaker in an introduction, especially if the chairman knows him well. However, this must never be done so that offense is taken. Moreover, when a chairman pokes fun at a speaker in some way it must unquestionably be recognized as fun. It may be followed with serious remarks commending the speaker.

5. When the speaker concludes, the chairman should express his appreciation.

The chairman may play a significant role in the success of any meeting by the thoughtful discharge of his responsibilities. The ability with which a chairman or toastmaster arranges an event, chooses a speaker, and handles the meeting will determine in a large measure whether those in attendance waste their time or profit from the meeting.

CHAPTER III

QUIPS AND WITTICISMS

An economist is a person who talks about something he doesn't understand and makes you believe you're ignorant.

An eager beaver is a person who works twice as hard but doesn't know why.

Most persons who get something for nothing are disappointed if they don't get more.

The greatest disadvantage in life is to have too many advantages.

To be frank is to tell the truth about anything that won't hurt you.

When you have trouble, you learn which friends have been waiting with a paddle to find you bent over.

Patience is the ability to stand something as long as it happens to the other fellow.

A scholar is a person with too much brains to be able to earn a large salary.

A socialist is an unsuccessful person who figures his last chance to get something is to get part of yours.

Tradition: The widespread acceptance of something which was at first of questionable merit — and still is.

Most women are as pretty this year as they were five years ago, but it takes quite a little longer.

Laughter is the sound you hear when you stumble, or lose your hat in the wind.

A library is a place where the dead live.

Genius is the ability to evade work by doing something right the first time it has been done.

Good judgment comes from experience and experience comes from poor judgment.

Under a planned economy the government encourages the farmers to raise a bumper crop so the government will have to buy a lot of the bumper crop to keep from having a bumper crop.

Sometimes we long for the good old days when all this country had to fear was an attack from the Indians.

Nothing is impossible. Now we have peace on a war basis.

The desire for fame is simply the desire to write your own epitaph.

Advice to the lovelorn is the bunk. If you're in love, you won't want it — or need it.

One good thing about growing old is that you don't have to go to picnics.

A necessary evil is one we like so much we refuse to do away with it.

Everyone wants to divide the wealth if he will get more than he has now.

Many a person who burned the candle at both ends would be satisfied with even a small flame now.

To win an argument one must always argue with someone who knows less than he does, but that isn't easy either.

On a street car or bus there is no such thing as the rising generation.

If you bow at all, give it all you've got.

Hope springs eternal in the shopper who looks for a ripe cantaloupe.

Time is what passes between pay days.

Many a man expects to be buried from the church but does nothing about keeping it open until his funeral gets there.

The course of true love isn't smooth, but the detours are worse.

If some people weren't stupid, how could we know who is intelligent.

At a dinner what's on the chairs is as important as what's on the table.

You can measure the progress of civilization by who gets more applause — the clown or the thinker.

It does your heart good to hear a small boy eat.

A vacation resort is where you go when you are worn out and where you come back from a complete wreck.

Pessimism is the determination to see less than there is in anything, and optimism is the ability to see more than there is in everything.

Politician's Re-election Slogan: Honesty is no substitute for experience.

No one is so hard to answer as a fellow who keeps his mouth shut.

When everyone approves of what you are doing, you ought to ask yourself what's wrong.

The more help I have in the garden, the more I like gardening.

The reason the road to success is crowded is that it is filled with women pushing their husbands.

Only the very rich can afford to be foolish, and not infrequently are.

Nothing is more difficult than trying to find something wrong with yourself.

Every new idea is an impossibility until it is born.

No person has really seen life until he has talked with the ticket seller in a theater box office.

After dinner coffee is never so pleasant as when it is mixed with a little gossip.

Many a successful person has risen from obscurity to something worse.

Think twice before you speak and you may say something even more aggravating.

Honesty pays but not enough to satisfy some people.

School boy's description of an elephant — 8,000 pounds of liver with legs.

The trouble in some marriages is that the women have husbands with extravagant wives. Or the men have wives with extravagant husbands.

The young man in love thinks nothing is good enough for the girl except himself.

If some people lived up to their ideals they would be stooping.

No one ought to be so pessimistic he can't see some good in the other fellow's troubles.

Sometimes we think everybody sees television but the fellow who writes the commercials.

There is somethnig comforting about the other fellow's hard luck.

The average husband is worth about twice what his wife thinks of him and half what his mother thinks of him.

The best speech you hear may be from the fellow who keeps his mouth shut.

Many a husband loves his wife still.

We live in a world of change, but it's hard to get your hands on any of it.

Only one American in two knows how to drive a car well, and she sits in the back seat.

Courage — Being brave when you know something isn't going to happen to you.

Executive — A person who can without the facts make quick decisions which occasionally are right.

Any married man who agrees with his wife can have his own way.

Most girls want a spendthrift before they're married and a man who has saved his money after they're married.

We never could understand how a moth lives by eating nothing but holes.

We have more high school and college graduates than ever before and fewer of them can read traffic signs.

We never get anything but sad news out of those envelopes with a window in front.

A fish gains weight slowly, except the one that got away.

Early to bed and early to rise, and you'll miss hearing and seeing a great deal that would make you wise.

Money talks and in most families it's the mother tongue.

"Hear no evil, see no evil, speak no evil," and you'll certainly be a dull companion.

All of us are born in a state of ignorance and many of us never change residence.

When you decide to know yourself, you may find the acquaintance isn't worth the effort.

Sometimes we think an enterchurch movement is more important than an interchurch movement.

Sometimes we like to go to an old fashioned silent movie and see people open their mouths without saying anything.

There are some Americans who are weary of well-doing, while others are weary of being well done.

The news from over the world is sometimes bad and sometimes even worse.

Some day we're going to give that Gideon Bible in our hotel room to the head waiter in the dining room.

It's a delicate problem to cultivate your friends so you know them well enough to borrow from but not well enough to lend to.

We suppose a fat man dressed up is an illustration of spic and span.

We like the fellow who says he is going to make a long story short, and does.

An automobile is only as fast as the people in it.

If you would like to be talked about, leave the party before the rest do.

We have seen some women who have discovered the secret of perpetual emotion.

Equality means every one is as good as everyone else, and generally better.

A woman doesn't have to be musical to get airs out of a mink coat.

A man is endowed with certain inalienable rights all of which he must fight for.

They were happily married, because she was his little treasure and he was her great big treasury.

The most effective answer to an insult is silence.

Man is superior because of all the animals only he survives the cruelty and greed of man.

Some movie stars diet to keep thin, but the movie plots stay that way.

A medical specialist is a man who wants all your teeth pulled before he tries another guess.

A fisherman is the only person who tells a lie with his arms stretched out.

No amount of misfortune will satisfy a man who reaches for a second hors d'oeuvre.

Nothing holds back progress like ignorance which is confident, and if it is enthusiastic also, it's unbeatable.

Man is peculiar. He will tortue animals but do nothing about a radio soprano or a singing commercial.

A person who says, "I'm not dumb", is merely trying to quiet his own doubts.

Why do we all want to talk about ourselves when that's the subject we know least about.

It's difficult to understand how a person can be bored with life and yet hope for immortality.

When a man doesn't believe today what he believed yesterday, how can he be so confident today knowing that tomorrow is coming.

Honesty is the best policy, but difficult to follow in a letter of recommendation.

The person who thinks before he speaks is silent most of the time.

When some people abuse you, they can't understand why you resent "constructive criticism".

When the cat is in the bird cage, he isn't there to sing.

Ignorance combined with silence is sometimes mistaken for wisdom.

Conversation without a touch of scandal gets very dull for most people.

Some persons think they aren't getting ahead unless they've cheated the other fellow.

No woman understands that even a bargain costs money.

Freedom of speech is a great thing. It even permits some people to talk nonsense.

It's difficult to define the word, "ignoramus", unless one has studied himself pretty carefully.

None but the brave can afford the fair.

We suggest that some new issue of postage stamps carry a picture of a weeping taxpayer.

We should think they could balance the French budget with the mistakes in addition in Paris cafes in one tourist season.

It is no sillier for the rich to think the poor are happy than for the poor to think the rich are.

The world's choice: Disarmament or Disbursement.

Nothing makes time pass more quickly than an income tax installment every three months.

June is the month when the bride who has never had a broom in her hand sweeps up the aisle.

We sympathize with the fellow who occupied two seats in the bus because half the time he didn't get any seat.

To be unhappily married requires a good income and to be incompatible a couple must be rich.

Adam was the first man to know the meaning of rib-roast.

Some persons never appeal to God unless they're getting licked.

To a Communist, a wage slave is any American who earns $10,000 a year, drives a car, owns a television set and has a bathroom.

Sometimes we think the wicked fleece and no man pursueth.

Man has conquered the air but so has our neighbor's radio.

Modern youngsters are precocious. They don't read, but name any record and they can tell you what's on the other side.

The Greeks had their idea of tragedy, but they never sat in the grandstand and watched an outfielder drop an easy one.

Most women have a skin they love to retouch.

It's strange that the fellow who always wants the most has the least with which to buy it.

You can't believe everything you hear, but you can repeat it.

Misfortune is a point of view. Your headache feels good to an aspirin salesman.

Some day some smart government is going to get the idea of spending only what it can pay for.

A national conscience is a still small voice that tells one country when another country is stronger.

One trouble is that nations are not only off the gold standard, but the golden rule standard.

Faint praise ne'er won fair lady, but it would certainly surprise many wives.

The little savings banks that couldn't be opened until they were full are now antiques.

"Heaven is not reached in a single bound", says the poet. It may be on a busy street corner.

Every young man knows when the right girl comes along because she tells him.

If ignorance is bliss, what's the sense of giving intelligence tests.

There must be something wrong in the world somewhere that doesn't need Uncle Sam's money.

As you grow older you find the after-dinner speeches get worse or your back weaker.

The person who is ignorant can speak freely.

A saver grows rich by seeming poor. A spender grows poor by seeming rich.

Men are either born with consciences or marry them.

A sense of humor helps some people get a laugh out of their friends' troubles.

Most of us are willing to follow the advice of our superiors if we can find any.

At international conferences we never seem to have any record of the still small voice.

People who offer good advice always offer it in the big economy size.

When you say you will do a job tomorrow, ask yourself what you did about it yesterday.

The person who offers us advice for our own good seldom does us any.

Many a man tumbles over his own bluff.

Narrow-minded people are a nuisance if you find your conscience agrees with what they say.

Man reaps what he sows unless he is an amateur gardener.

Husbands are said to be more honest than bachelors. They have to be.

When you criticise your child for not being smart, remember a wooden head is one thing that can be inherited.

We are not certain whether people are getting worse or whether the newspapers keep us better informed.

Next to a clear conscience nothing beats a good lawyer.

What this country needs is some social workers to look after broken down tax payers.

Money makes fools of famous people, but it also makes famous people of fools.

Times change. In the old days you made $5 and spent $10. Now you make $25 and spend $50.

Experience keeps a dear school, but fools don't learn there either.

Why does a woman apologize when friends drop in unexpectedly and find the house looking like it usually does.

When both a speaker and an audience are confused, the speech is profound.

With lunch counters in every kind of store, you can eat almost anywhere except at home.

Where do bad boys and girls go? Just about everywhere.

The family Bible can be passed from generation to generation because it gets so little wear.

He was the kind of thoughtful person who never forgot himself.

Indigestion happens when there has been too much of a good thing.

One way to find out what a woman really thinks of you is to marry her.

Many a husband goes to his church rummage sale to buy back his Sunday pants.

Nobody knows who invented the alarm clock, which is certainly a fortunate break for the guy.

We have a peace-loving world with nations seldom paying pensions for more than three wars at a time.

A city farmer is a fellow who is willing to lose money farming if he can wear overalls.

Don't criticise the rooster. If you got up at 4 A. M., you'd crow too.

We can't remember of hearing of a man, when we were young, who hoed potatoes until he was a nervous wreck.

We'll never have a labor government in this country until cabinet salaries are up to the union scale.

Man is the only animal that punishes his fellows and perhaps the only one that should.

A free country is one in which no one in particular is to blame for the messes you get in.

Fortunately there are always enough crises in the world to help us keep our minds off our personal problems.

A civilized nation is one in which you decrease the death rate by disease and increase it by accident.

If you can buy a house for nothing down, you don't have to stay home to get your money's worth.

If you don't like worms, what's the sense of being the early bird?

A republic is a government in which those who don't vote criticise those who are elected.

About the time the bedtime stories are televised, many youngsters are going out for the evening.

Some families go right on putting money in a savings account or government bonds when they haven't got a mink coat in the house.

Many a man who doesn't play golf can't give it up.

Nothing is cuter than a little baby after the company is gone.

In many elections some good candidates get the solid support of all the good people who don't vote.

Without a single exception, we have always found that the narrow-minded bigots are the ones who disagree with us.

The world would be pretty bad if the teen-agers didn't have any more sense than we sometimes think they have.

Solomon said, "There is no new thing under the sun", but he didn't say it over color television.

Still, if there were no Communists, how could the Western nations scare themselves into being friends.

The summer tourist soon finds that the cheaper rooms in the beach hotel overlook the ocean — completely.

When someone says, "I do not wish to appear critical", it means he is going to let you have it,

Economics lesson: Increased earnings always bring increased yearnings.

A psychologist says if a child is naughty you should switch his attention. How's that?

You can't tell by the looks of a mink coat how many instalments are past due.

With some married couples the big difference of opinion is whether he earns too little or she spends too much.

Public opinion is simply the private opinion of one person who made enough noise to attract some converts.

This generation can drive automobiles, fly jet planes, and develop color television, but has trouble with juvenile delinquency.

There are a great many books now on how to live longer but none on why.

The fact that Congress is no better and no worse than the country is something to worry about.

The children run about everything now but the lawn mower and the vacuum cleaner.

Friendship is what makes you think almost as much of someone else as you do of yourself.

The person who always insists on speaking his mind doesn't necessarily have one.

A politician who says he will stick to the facts has no respect for tradition.

The person who has too much money for his own good easily finds friends to share his misfortune.

If every mischievous little boy got his reward in the end, we might do away with juvenile delinquency.

Some housewives run charge accounts with four grocers because it makes the bills seem smaller.

If the Spring poets want to be realistic, they should find more words that rhyme with slush.

Success in life generally expands the waistband or the hatband.

If we didn't have confidence in each other, we couldn't live beyond our incomes.

Some successful men who have air-conditioned offices were reared in homes where the snow blew in through chinks in the attic.

We have never heard anyone say he couldn't sleep last night because of his conscience.

If you can't find it in the dictionary, the atlas or the encyclopedia, ask for it at the drug store.

Prosperity is the period when it is easy to borrow money to buy things which you should be able to pay for out of your own income.

The five B's of middle age — baldness, bridgework, bifocals, baywindows and bunions.

Scientists may gradually increase man's life so he will live to be 100 years. This is going to give the installment business a big boost.

There are times when we think that the plural of whim is women.

It is getting so a good barber can earn as much per word as an author.

When the Secretary of the Treasury tries to sleep, we suppose he counts his sheep in billions.

Experience is not only a dear teacher, but by the time you get through going to her school, life is over.

You can judge a man pretty well by whether he would ask for a light burden or a strong back if he were given a choice.

When a wife buys on credit, she is merely displaying confidence in her husband.

People go on vacations to forget things. When they open their bags, they find out what they are.

Seems like most everybody's looking for less to do, more time to do it in, and more pay for not doing it.

There are still a number of things you can get for a dollar, like nickles, dimes and quarters.

Critic's comment about a play: The scenery was beautiful, but the actors got in front of it.

Flattery is the art of telling someone exactly what he thinks of himself.

The best way to tell a woman's age is in a whisper.

No one so thoroughly appreciates the value of constructive criticism as the one giving it.

There comes a time in the life of every youth when he wonders how such dull parents could beget such a bright child.

In the business world an executive knows something about everything, the technician knows everything about something, and the switchboard operator knows everything.

Every year it seems to take less time to fly across the ocean and longer to drive to work.

Marriage: The alliance of two people, one who never remembers birthdays and the other who never forgets them.

It wasn't so long ago that women had to carry in the wash water from the well, but at least they didn't have to lay awake nights trying to figure out how to make the payments on the old wash tub.

Waiter: One who believes that money grows on trays.

Satellite: An ambitious employee at a party the boss gives.

We have tried but we have never been successful in making laws that keep us from making fools of ourselves.

Some times we miss happiness by looking too far for things near by.

Aren't there some times when you would prefer it if people didn't tell the truth about you?

Most people will agree with you if you keep quiet.

One way to reach old age is to quit feeling responsible for the entire world.

If you are too busy to feel miserable, you will be happy.

A man who is on a wild goose chase all his life never feathers much of a nest.

No conceited person is allergic to a mirror.

If you think you know it all, you haven't been listening.

It is always easy to see the silver lining in the other person's cloud.

Some times you find a person who knows how to live everyone's life expertly but his own.

The fact that no one knows anything about the future makes economic forecasting easy.

It's almost impossible to keep from telling others how much you know.

It is difficult to realize that a person who doesn't take your advice may not be stubborn.

A fool and his money get to go places.

Some persons would rather be wrong than quiet.

America has some fine old ruins and you can always see some of them at cocktail parties.

You have to be pretty smart in order to see your duty in time to avoid it.

One thing the members of the United Nations have is the ability to see each other's faults clearly.

Some people are always in debt because they keep spending what their friends think they make.

All things come to him who waits, but not soon enough to do much good.

Some persons won't suffer in silence because that would take the pleasure out of it.

A good wife always helps her husband with the work around the house.

No one has his ups and downs like the person who gets the aisle seat at the theater and arrives early.

A scientist says life is the metabolic activity of protoplasm, but it seems worse than that on Monday morning.

If you can remember the days when most persons had a conscience, you are getting old.

You are young only once but can be immature all your life.

A fool and his money are welcome as long as it lasts.

Many persons who didn't save last month are certain they will next month.

Few persons ever grow up. They merely change their playthings.

It's almost impossible to succeed if you cannot do what you are told — or can do nothing else.

It's a man's world, but the property is in his wife's name.

It makes a lot of difference in life whether you live and learn or just live.

A person who is alone isn't necessarily in good company.

A bore is a person who is me-deep in his conversation.

Only a few people live on borrowed time compared to the number who live on borrowed money.

Always put off until tomorrow the things you shouldn't do at all.

Your home town is where the people wonder how in the world you got as far as you did.

Destiny may shape our ends but making ends meet is our responsibility.

The still small voice used to be your conscience, but now it's your pocket radio.

Loafer: A person who sees a completed job and is certain he could have done it better.

We all want to live a long time but no one wants to get old.

The fellow who watches the clock need not worry about his future because he probably hasn't any.

Financial success: An accomplishment that helps you to see your relatives frequently.

Big head: The sign of a small man.

The United States is the one country where it takes more brains to make out the income tax return than it does to make the income.

Often the most wonderful thing wives can do with left-overs is to throw them out.

It's surprising how many persons our age are a lot older than we are.

Some persons want the benefit of doubt when there isn't any.

It isn't easy for a husband to get back some of his take-home pay after he takes it home.

Work is time you spend on jobs you get paid for and leisure is time you spend on jobs you don't get paid for.

Love your enemy and it will completely confuse him.

In middle age you are as young as ever but it takes a lot more effort.

A cat doesn't have nine lives but catty remarks do.

The thing for a husband to do when he spills something on a rug at home is merely to listen.

It isn't easy to get an idea into a head filled with prejudices.

Memory is the thing you have to forget with.

Some people think life is dull if there isn't any place to go where they shouldn't be.

Some persons jump at conclusions while others dig for facts.

One of the great mysteries to a married man is what a bachelor does with his time and money.

There are one or two countries so backward the people don't spend money until they have saved it.

A bachelor is a man with enough confidence in women to act on it.

If people said what they thought, our conversation would be very brief.

Occasionally you meet a person whose only job is spreading ignorance.

One thing about getting old is that you can sing in the bath-room while brushing your teeth.

The world isn't getting smaller. The missiles just go further.

A pessimist on world conditions had insomnia so bad the sheep were picketing him for shorter hours.

Laziness is the love of calm and peace.

Even a person who serves as a horrible example for others isn't entirely useless.

The three balls in front of a pawn shop mean it's two to one you don't get it back.

If a man has so much money he doesn't know his son is in college, he is well to do.

One trouble with the country is that you can't pass enough laws to keep people from making fools of themselves.

The person who tells his dollars where to go saves money, and the person who wants to know where they went doesn't.

Listening to advice may get you into trouble, but it makes the other person feel better.

It's strange, but you may try to do something and fail and try to do nothing and succeed.

There may be some consolation in the fact that the dollar you haven't got isn't worth so much as it was.

A scientist says the world will last a billion years longer, which doesn't help our present pessimism about world affairs.

The persons who live next door listen to both sides of a family argument.

We are looking for a book on "How to Avoid Doing It Yourself."

Never invest in a sure thing unless you have money to lose.

Blue jeans: What people used to wear who worked.

All play and no work makes it difficult to know what to do with your leisure.

The trouble with the nations today is that they all want to play the big drum and no one wants to play second fiddle.

The world is getting smaller but it costs more to run it.

Under privileged: Not to have remote control for your color television set.

Civilization is not only at the crossroads, but this is a cloverleaf job.

Women keep a secret well but sometimes it takes quite a few of them to do it.

A person who is articulate and ignorant is certain to go a long way.

We like the person who tells us all the nice things about ourselves that we always knew.

What this country needs is a cheap substitute for money and it may get it.

It's sad to have loved and lost, but it is cheaper.

If you want a knot on your head, put a chip on your shoulder.

Money has wings and most of us see only the tail feathers.

Tourist: A person who drives 1,000 miles to see some beautiful scenery and litters the road all the way.

Executive: A person who never even dreamed of earning the salary he can't get along on today.

The news from over the world is sometimes bad and sometimes even worse.

Some persons never appeal to God unless they are getting licked.

A taxpayer is a person who has the whole government on his payroll.

Adolescence is the period when children are certain they will never be as stupid as their parents.

Money may not bring happiness but it would be nice to find out for yourself.

If a man has a wife who tells him what to do and a secretary who does it he may be a success.

When a woman marries now, she gets a husband and domestic help.

Sign on the door of a bankrupt retail store: "Opened by mistake."

Rush hour: When the traffic stands still.

Dollars and sense go together.

Money talks but in inflation it doesn't have enough cents to say anything worthwhile.

Count down on the money in your pocket book — fifty-forty-thirty-twenty-ten-zero — and there she goes until next pay day.

Success is relative, and the more you have of it the more relatives.

It's hard to believe that someone can differ with us and be right.

With a load of instalment payments the Joneses probably have a tough time keeping up with themselves.

No wonder the grocery bill is high when you see all those nylons, cosmetics and records your wife bought at the supermarket.

Occasionally you meet a person who thinks that if he hadn't been born people would wonder why.

We imagine a youngster of eighteen who thinks he will grow up to be as dumb as his parents must get pretty discouraged.

If you didn't make mistakes you might live and die without ever hearing your name mentioned.

Some women have only three requirements for a husband — money, wealth and property.

If ignorance is bliss, what's the sense of intelligence tests.

One advantage about baldness is that it requires very little attention.

People who offer good advice always offer it in the big economy size.

It's only on matters of great principle that some people lie with a clear conscience.

Faint praise ne'er won fair lady, but it would certainly surprise many wives.

It's good to have an open mind if you know what to let in.

When you buy on the instalment plan you don't need a calendar.

Half a loafer is better than a whole loafer.

Egotist: A person of low taste, more interested in himself than in me.

Quartet: Four people who think the same thing — that the other three can't sing.

Punctuality: The art of guessing how late the other fellow is going to be.

It's surprising how many persons unselfishly will neglect their own work in order to tell you how to run your affairs.

If you want to be popular, you have to listen while people tell you a lot of things you already know.

A rooster crows early in the morning because he probably can't get in a word after the hens get up.

Next to automation nothing beats a waste basket for speeding up work.

The driver who blows his horn often gets the right of way and the fellow who just blows often does so also.

Patrick Henry said, "Give me liberty or give me death", but now we leave out the words liberty and death.

Early to bed and early to rise is a sure sign that you don't care for television.

Nothing gives you quite the thrill of treading in the darkness on a step that isn't there.

Remember the old days when people killed time by working instead of by coffee breaks.

The longest way home is on the old expense account.

If you make a better mousetrap now, you're just in the old rat race.

In the old days child guidance was something parents were expected to provide and not submit to.

The reason some of us find it difficult to think is that we haven't had any previous experience.

In the good old days you paddled your own canoe but now an outboard motor does it for you.

A good many car drivers don't need seat belts as much as they need straitjackets.

A gentleman is a man who leaves the lawn mower and garden tools out where his wife can find them.

When a person feels that his thinking is getting broader, it is more likely that his conscience is stretching.

A big man is not one who makes no mistakes, but one who is bigger than any mistakes he makes.

Many best sellers in modern fiction are divisible into three types — neurotic, erotic, and tommyrotic.

The average is merely the poorest of the good and the best of the bad. Maybe now we'll quit boasting about being "average."

The person who invented motels has them strategically located so you go by the best ones between 7 :00 A. M. and noon.

A foreigner commented, "You Americans are strange people. You devote one day out of the year to your mothers and a whole week to pickles."

Thrift is a virtue that we wish our ancestors had practised more of so that so much of it wouldn't be forced on us now.

Neck: Something which if you don't stick out, you won't get into trouble up to.

One trouble with the world is that there are too many clowns who aren't in the circus.

Some people are always taking the joy out of life and a good many of them are in the Internal Revenue Department.

A man hasn't really tested his strength until he tries to lift a mortgage.

Why don't life's problems hit us when we are eighteen and know everything?

There are few husbands who do not love their wives still.

Advice from an old carpenter: Measure twice and saw once.

Americans take good care of their cars and also keep pedestrians in good running condition.

Those who complain about the way the ball bounces are often the ones who dropped it.

We understand there's a car so compact that, when the carburetor is flooded, you can throw it over your shoulder and burp it.

It would be a great relief to live in that town on television where the hero always finds a parking place in front of the bank, the supermarket, and the post office.

We've made great medical progress in the last generation. What used to be merely an itch is now an allergy.

Popular expressions are sometimes misleading. They call it the "rush hour" aroud 5 o'clock, when you sit in your car for half an hour waiting for the traffic to move twelve feet.

After all is said and done, more is said than done.

Take an ordinary party and remove the chairs, and you have a reception.

There are some people who not only keep you from being lonely, but make you wish you were.

Memory is what keeps telling you that you know the guy without giving you any idea of who he is.

For fixing things around the house, nothing beats a man who's handy with a checkbook.

One good thing about inflation is that it's practically impossible for a youngster to get sick on a 5-cent candy bar.

Salary is an amount of money that, no matter how large it is, some people spend more than.

Neurotic: A person who suffers from causes for which there is no known disease.

Dentist: A person you see when your toothache drives you to extraction.

When you see a man with a woman who looks young enough to be his daughter, it could be his mother.

"We'll advise you in due course" means "if we figure it out, we'll let you know."

To err is human, but to admit it is not.

The world is so full of a number of things that it's hard to keep up with the payments on them.

Unimpeachable source: The person who started the rumor originally.

Traffic light: A little green light that changes to red as your car approaches.

Ant: A small insect which is always at work but still finds time to go to picnics.

Mealtime, as one overworked mother put it, is when the kids sit down to continue eating.

Seeing ourselves as others see us wouldn't do much good. We would not believe what we saw.

After all is said and done, it's usually the wife who has said it and the husband who has done it.

The church service is not a convention to which a family should merely send a delegate.

Lie: An aversion to the truth.

Angle: A triangle with only two sides.

Counter irritant: A person who shops all day and buys nothing.

If at first you succeed, you probably haven't accomplished much.

All that stops most of us from having a nervous breakdown these days is that we can't afford it.

Anybody who thinks that money grows on trees is bound, sooner or later, to get caught out on a limb.

Some people are not the life of the party until they leave.

Baby sitter, greeting the returning parents: "Don't apologize. I wouldn't be in a hurry to come home either!"

Three meals a day, a roof over my head, two cars, a boat, a power mower, and a contented wife — why shouldn't I be in debt?

The hardest dollar a fellow ever earned is the one he has already spent.

A good wife always helps her husband with the work around the house.

The only fool bigger than the one who knows it all is one who will argue with him.

All things come to him who waits, but not soon enough to do much good.

One thing the members of the United Nations have is the ability to see each other's faults clearly.

You have to be pretty smart in order to see your duty in time to avoid it.

America has some fine old ruins and you can always see some of them at cocktail parties.

It is difficult to realize that a person who doesn't take your advice may not be stubborn.

It's almost impossible to keep from telling others how much you know.

The fact that no one knows anything about the future makes economic forecasting easy.

No conceited person is allergic to a mirror.

There is no such thing as an idle rumor.

A person may watch TV westerns every night and still be perfectly sane in other ways.

CHAPTER IV

UNUSUAL ILLUSTRATIONS

CREED FOR AMERICANS

I believe in America because in it we are free — free to choose our government, to speak our minds, to observe our different religions.

Because we are generous with our freedom, we share our rights with those who disagree with us.

Because we hate no people and covet no peoples' lands.

Because we are blessed with a natural and varied abundance.

Because we have great dreams and because we have the opportunity to make those dreams come true.

Wendell L. Willkie

IN THE GOOD OLD DAYS

About 100 years ago, the Pony Express recruited for riders with this advertisement:

"Wanted — young skinny wiry fellows not over 18. Must be expert riders willing to risk death daily. Orphans preferred. Wages, $25 a week."

SUCCESS

An American can consider himself a success when it costs him more to support the government than to support a wife and children. *Automotive Dealer News*

THE LATER YEARS

A recent analysis of achievements of 400 famous men throughout history is highly encouraging to all who think they are growing old.

The study revealed that more than one-third achieved their greatest accomplishments after they passed the age of 60. A surprising 23 per cent scored their greatest success in life after the age of 70.   *Quote*

WRITING FOR ETERNITY

Thomas Mann always works on each book for a very long time. Even when the manuscript is supposedly ready, he continues to work on it. When he kept on changing things in *Magic Mountain,* his publisher finally called him up and wailed: "We'll never get this book out! You've been working on it for eternity!"

"After all," was his calm reply, "I'm writing it for eternity."   *Munich Revue*

ON ANY STREET

People on any street appear upon trivial errands, but their looks are misleading. For in the jostling throng there is a boy headed for his draft board, another for a physician's office to learn the results of a medical test; there is a new widow, and next to her a woman seeking a divorce; there is a lonely girl meeting a stranger down town, and behind her a girl going to confessional; there is a couple trying to borrow money for the downpayment on property and another family picking out a casket.   *Harlan Miller*

IN THE OLD DAYS

One vacationer reports seeing a sign in a restaurant as follows: "Pies like mother used to make before she took up bridge and cigarettes."

THOMAS JEFFERSON

Thomas Jefferson, in the epitaph which he composed for his own gravestone, neglected to mention the fact that he once had been President of the United States! He did, however, state that he was the author of the Declaration of Independence and of the Statute of Virginia for Religious Freedom, and that he was the founder of the University of Virginia.

CONTENTMENT IN NATURE

When I would beget content, and increase confidence in the power and wisdom and providence of Almighty God, I will walk the meadows by some gliding stream, and there contemplate the lilies that take no care, and those very many other little living creatures that are not only created, but fed (man knows not how) by the goodness of the God of Nature, and therefore trust in Him.   *Izaak Walton*

AND ROBOTS TO EAT IT?

Authorities predict that before long American housewives will make an audio record on tape of the menu for the day. The tape, at a precise time, will set in motion devices that will defrost the frozen food, place it in an infrared electric oven, and deliver it to the table.

TOO LATE!

He always said he would retire when he made a million clear. And so he toiled into the dusk from day to day, from year to year.

At last, he put his ledgers up and laid his stock reports aside, but when he started out to live, he found he had already died.   *Sunshine Magazine*

BIG ORDER — FEW WORDS

When you contemplate the longwinded letters and memoranda that clutter up the files of most business organizations, you may possibly do something to lessen the mess in your own files if you will remember the order said to have been given to General Eisenhower by General Marshall as the former prepared to leave for Europe. On a small memorandum sheet addressed to Eisenhower appeared these words: "Proceed to London. Invade continent. Destroy the enemy Army."

AS IN THE DAYS OF ROME

Very few people ever take time to read such masterpieces as Edward Gibbon's *Decline and Fall of the Roman Empire,* but to read this particular work is worthwhile for the picture contained therein of the world today. Those who have thought that one of the greatest empires ever built by man fell because of the invasion of the virile people from the North — the Huns, the Goths, and the Vandals, who came sweeping down on Rome and laid waste the great Eternal City — are mistaken, according to Gibbon.

"No," proclaims Gibbon, "that did not cause the fall of the Roman Empire; that was merely a circumstance of the fall." The reasons he enumerates for the fall of the empire were these: The rapid increase in divorce, undermining the sanctity and dignity of the home; higher and higher taxes to pay for bread and circuses to gain the support of the masses for a totalitarian government; the mad desire for pleasure — pleasure that was becoming indecent; piling weapons upon weapons when the real enemies were within; the decay of religious faith, so that religion became a hollow form.

"These," says Gibbon, "are the reasons for the decay and decline of the Roman Empire" — and every one of them is a great and terrible reality to deal with in the world today, and particularly, it seems, in the United States. Does this mean that American civilization has attained its zenith and is about to experience a decline or a complete breakdown? Herein, certainly, is cause for concern.

Adapted from PEO Record

OAKS OR SQUASHES

When James Garfield (later President of the United States) was principal of Hiram College in Ohio, a father asked him if the course of study couldn't be simplified so that his son might be able to "go through by a shorter route."

"Certainly," Garfield replied. "But it all depends upon what you want to make of your boy. When God wants to make an oak tree, He takes a hundred years. When He wants to make a squash, He requires only two months."

We are producing too many squashes and not enough oak trees in our day. The verbs we most commonly use give us away: we "leap" out of bed; we "gulp" our coffee; we "bolt" our food; we "whizz" into town; we "dash" to the office; we "tear" for home; and we "drop" dead! Our age is one of anxiety, impatience, aimlessness; of panaceas, quick cures, and shortcuts; of ulcers and crackups and breakdowns. Almost the first words a youngster hears as he begins to toddle are: "C'mon, hurry up!" And ever after Mom and Pop and teacher and coach all unite in reminding him that, if he is "going to get anywhere in life," he'd better "get a move on."

Perhaps Pascal had something when, centuries ago, he said: "All the troubles of man come from his not knowing how to sit still." When whirl is King, chaos is his Kingdom. When haste makes waste, it is the more important values that are lost, until soon we are lost ourselves, in what T. S. Eliot properly called "A Waste Land." Then life is bereft of its purpose, and loses its zest and thrill. Then people are like flies on a dizzy flywheel, going like the wind but only going in circles. Is it any wonder that the psychiatrist gets many of us, and most of the rest of us just escape by the skin of our teeth?

Angus J. MacQueen, Moderator of the General Council of The United Church of Canada

THE IMPORTANCE OF EXAMPLE

Willa Cather wrote a book a few years ago called "Shadows on the Rock." She tells so well the story of Father Hector, a polished scholar who became a missionary to the Huron Indians, and his friend, the apothecary Auclair. The apothecary says to Father Hector, in one of the scenes, while they were at dinner, "Next Autumn we are returning to France. I expect you to go with us." Father Hector replied, "Ah, no. Thank you, but no. I have taken a vow that will spoil your plans for me. I shall not return to France." The apothecary is shocked and calls to Father Hector's memory that this is the plan of which they talked while his wife was there. Then Father Hector speaks again. "Listen, my friend. No man can give himself heart and soul to one thing while in the back of his mind he cherishes a desire, a secret hope, for something very different. You as a student must know that even in worldly affairs nothing worth while is accomplished except by that last sacrifice, the giving of oneself altogether and finally. Since I made that final sacrifice, I have been twice the man I was before." Auclair says, "You have made a vow, you say? Is it irrevocable?" Father Hector replies, "Irrevocable. And what do you suppose gave me the strength to make that decision? Why merely a good example."

Then follows the story of the example which prompted Father Hector to take this strange vow, as strange today amidst a group of vacillating Christians as in the pioneer days of the story. Father Hector related an incident in the life of Father Chabanel, one of the early missionaries to the Indians. He had come to Canada from "the gracious city of Toulouse." His had been a life of ease, luxury, and softness. His scholarship was of the best, his love for the sophisticated life of France real. Although a master of Hebrew and Greek, Italian and Spanish, he found himself unable to master the language of the Indians. The utter poverty and vulgarity of life around him nauseated him, the Indians rebuked him, until he could stand it no more and asked to be released. The greatest struggle was spiritual, for, "the greatest suffering was an almost continual sense of the withdrawal of God." The time had come for Father Chabanal's return to France, when "on Corpus Christi Day, in the fifth year of his labours in Canada and the thirty-fifth of his age, he cut short this struggle and overcame his temptation. At the mission of Saint Matthias, in the presence of the Blessed Sacrament exposed, he made a vow of perpetual stability (perpetuam stabilitatem) in the Huron Missions." "This," Father Hector said, "I have done, and the vow of perpetual stability taken by Father Chabanel has become mine, and I am staying in Canada, never to return to my beloved France."

Somewhere, and soon, take a vow of perpetual stability to the things that are vital in religion; and then by your example, you may influence others in the faith.

Wilbur Frank Dierking, Minister, The Union Church of Rio de Janeiro, Rio de Janeiro, Brazil

SMILE WHEN YOU ASK THAT

Vice President Johnson recently went to the Willard Hotel, which refers to itself as the hotel of the Presidents, to attend a luncheon for George Dixon, the wit and humor columnist, marking the publication of Dixon's entertaining book, "Leaning on a Column."

When he was unable to find the luncheon because it was not listed on the hotel's bulletin board, Johnson approached a young woman at the reception desk.

"I am the Vice President," he began.

The young woman flashed her most engaging smile and sweetly inquired, "May I ask of what?"

ONE NIGHT ON THE MOUNT OF OLIVES

Some time ago I spent a number of weeks in the countries of the Far East and the Middle East.

One afternoon I flew from Beirut past the Sea of Galilee and the historic city of Damascus, over the rolling hills of Judea to the City of Jerusalem. That night I stood on the top of the Mount of Olives. Only a short distance away were the lights of the little village of Bethany, and on beyond in the distance were the faint and flickering lights of Jericho, where today they are excavating the old City of Jericho, the oldest city known to man.

To the right was the Dead Sea, and the brilliant radiance of a full moon illuminated a broad path across its calm waters. In the cliffs along that sea, scholars today are finding some of the most fabulous manuscripts which have ever been uncovered describing early civilizations.

As I looked across the countryside, I thought of the tens of thousands of wretched and restless refugees camping in those barren valleys below. I also looked that night across thousands of miles and saw again the huddled masses and the hungry millions of Pakistan and India. Even further to the East, not far from Hong Kong, I saw once more the Chinese peasant women ankle deep in the flooded rice paddies near the boundary of Red China, reaching down into the mud and plowing it with their own hands. Over the vast area of Southern Asia, hundreds of millions of men and women have now won a new independence and are engaged in a desperate and determined struggle to grow strong, with all this implies to the future of Western civilization.

I went a few feet and looked in the other direction down the barren, rocky slope of the Mount of Olives over the dark, gnarled and old olive trees where the Garden of Gethsemane had been. Just across a little valley a few blocks in width were the lights of Jerusalem on the opposite hill.

That night I looked down through the centuries. There was the place where Solomon — who it is said "exceeded all the kings of the earth in riches and in wisdom" — had built his temple. There was the place where many of the heroic figures of Jewish history — Abraham and Isaac and David — had walked, where Christianity was born, and where many of the ideals of Western civilization had been cradled.

On that hill, Herod, too, had built his temple, and the authorities of the Roman Government had once ruled in all their majesty, when the Roman Empire had flung its legions to those remote frontiers. But Rome fell at the time when it had the greatest armies and the most powerful fortifications in its history, but also when it had disintegrated and decayed at the heart.

Other great empires rose and fell — Spain and Portugal, France and the Netherlands. In this generation we have witnessed the decline in power of a great empire upon which the sun for generations had never set.

Now another power is striding majestically across the horizon of world affairs. Its armies, its planes, its ships, its money, its merchandise, and its financial genius are moving to the remote parts of the world. Lest we forget, every great nation which has risen to power has declined. In a world where two-thirds of the people have annual incomes of less than one hundred dollars a year, we are richer than any nation in history has ever been. The call of economic comfort is loud. But are the objectives today of leisure instead of labor, of demands instead of duties, of spending instead of saving — are these the earmarks of an advancing civilization, or are they the evidences of disintegrating character?

One can only hope that the courage, integrity, and valiant spirit that rode the adventurous *Mayflower* in the storm-swept Atlantic, built log cabins in the rocky hills of New England, and with unbelievable hardship blazed trails across the wide plains in covered wagons to stake out a new nation, are somehow secure and sheltered deep in the hearts of the American people.   *Herbert V. Prochnow*

HENRY'S TOY

Of the many stories which have become a part of the American saga surrounding the life of Henry Ford, this one clearly shows the humble background of his life which helped to make him so great a figure in American tradition:

Henry Ford's first machine going by its own power, he called a "quadricycle," because of its four wheels. When it was finished, and had been tested to make sure it would run, he invited a friend to ride with him out to his father's farm to show his achievement.

Now Henry's father was a farmer, a believer in horses, a man of position in the neighborhood, a justice of the peace, and a Baptist deacon. As Henry proudly drove through the farm gate to where his father and a neighbor were standing in the lot, they just stared — speechless! Every line in his father's face indicated shame and humiliation that Henry, a grown man, should still be playing with toys. The older man never said a word, only looked his displeasure.

When Henry could endure his father's disdain no longer, he turned to his friend and said, "Come on, let's you and me get out of here," and he drove back through the big gate to the road.   *P. E. O. Record*

CHILDREN

On the occasion of the celebration of his 80th birthday anniversary, Herbert Hoover said this:

"The older I grow, the more I appreciate children. Now, at my 80th birthday, I salute them again. Children are the most wholesome part of the race, the sweetest, for they are freshest from the hand of God. Whimsical, ingenious, mischievous, they fill the world with joy and good humor. We adults live a life of apprehension as to what they will think of us; a life of defense against their terrifying energy; a life of hard work to live up to their great expectations. We put them to bed with a sense of relief — and greet them in the morning with delight and anticipation. We envy them the freshness of adventure and the discovery of life. In all these ways, children add to the wonder of being alive. In all these ways, they help to keep us young."

BENJAMIN FRANKLIN

Benjamin Franklin, who has many other claims to fame, was the first Postmaster-General of the United States, having been appointed by his good friend, President George Washington. Many phases of the present-day postal service were first conceived and put into operation by Franklin. He received a salary of $1,000 per year as head of the country's postal service.

THE MIDNIGHT RIDE

Once upon a time Henry Wadsworth Longfellow wrote a poem which immortalized "The Midnight Ride of Paul Revere." Mr. Revere was made extremely famous, and many are surprised when informed that there were two other men equally historically involved in that midnight affair. All three watched at the Old North Church for the signal which sent them galloping away to arouse their countrymen. Few know that the other two men who rode that night were William Dawes and Samuel Prescott.

It is a trite conclusion that to those who do not know us, we do not exist. Longfellow "advertised" the name of Paul Revere through his famous poem. The other two men were almost forgotten except for mention in a few history books.

BETTER THAN A BELL

It is told that the city fathers of Franklin, Massachusetts, wrote to Benjamin Franklin: "We have named our town after you, and we should like a donation of a sum of money from you in order to put a bell in the church steeple."

The erudite Franklin replied: "I am very much honored, very glad indeed to send you a sum of money; only don't buy a bell with it. Buy a library, because I have always preferred sense to sound."

They bought the books.

OPPORTUNITY IS SOMEWHERE ELSE

An Indian princess, when she came of age, was given a basket, and told that she might pick the finest ears of corn in a given row. The only requirement was that she was to choose as she went along — she could not retrace her steps.

She admired the fine quality of the corn before her; and as she felt one ear after another, she left them on the stalks, always thinking that better ears lay ahead. Suddenly, to her dismay, she came to the end of the row — and she had gathered none of them!   *Pipe Dreams*

HOW THEY GOT THAT WAY

John D. Rockefeller, Sr., who made untold millions of dollars during his lifetime, and became the world's richest man, started life hoeing potatoes at four cents an hour.

Lawrence Tibbett, internationally famous Metropolitan Opera star, first saw the inside of that building from the space reserved for standing room only, for which he paid $2.20, because he couldn't afford to buy a seat.

Charles Dickens received absolutely nothing for his first nine stories which were published. He received the equivalent of only five dollars for his tenth story.

THAT'S ENOUGH

→ Two secretaries were discussing their problems over a cup

of coffee. One of them said, "All I asked the boss was, 'Do you want the carbon copy double spaced too?' "

The Garber Rotarian, Garber, Oklahoma

YOUR TELEPHONE AGE

You can tell a person's age by his reaction to the telephone.

Youth. It can't ring without your being sure it's for you, with exciting news.

Late 20's, 30's and 40's. Hopeful anticipation, increasingly giving way to annoyance.

The 50's and 60's. You hope it's the wrong number and that no one wants you to do anything.

The 70's — Let someone else answer it — it won't be for you anyhow, thank goodness!

TWO IN ONE

When Robert Louis Stevenson wrote "Dr. Jekyll and Mr. Hyde," he harped upon a universal string, for every man has intermingled within him the high and the low, the beautiful and the unsightly, the angelic and the bestial, the laughter and the tears, the sunlight and the shadows of life. Every man's life is a battleground where virtue grapples with vileness, where the beacons of conscience seek to vanquish the legions of man's erring nature. Man is a two-fold being in whom the valleys of evil align themselves against the mountains of purity and seek to becloud their summits.

The outcome of this battle in the soul is highly important to the welfare of the individual. Should the lower nature of man emerge victorious from the strife, man will find himself groping in the morasses and midnight of life.

But if his higher nature wins, he will be elevated in spirit to the mountain-peaks of an enriched life, while the sunlight of virtue envelopes him and darkness holds no fears.

Each man may determine within himself where the feet of his spirit shall walk.   *Leo Bennett in Sunshine Magazine*

SIGN IN A GENERAL MOTORS FACTORY

According to the theory of aerodynamics and as may be readily demonstrated through wind tunnel experiments, the bumblebee is unable to fly. This is because the size, weight and shape of his body in relation to the total wingspread make flying impossible. BUT THE BUMBLEBEE, BEING IGNORANT OF THESE SCIENTIFIC TRUTHS, GOES AHEAD AND FLIES ANYWAY — AND MAKES A LITTLE HONEY EVERY DAY.

WHAT WILL THE NEIGHBORS SAY?

There is a story of Daniel Webster, well authenticated and worth the telling. After a long and arduous session of the Senate he had returned to his home in Boston, and, quite worn out, gave orders that in no circumstances was he to be disturbed.

Now it happened that he had scarcely reached his room and prepared to retire when some men from the little town in New Hampshire which had been his boyhood home called and said they must see Mr. Webster, that a man's life was at stake.

They had come to Boston as friends of a youth from the Senator's old home, who, as they believed, was falsely charged with murder. There was only one man in the nation, as they saw it, who could save the boy, and he was Daniel Webster.

The olive-complexioned statesman came downstairs, his face darker than usual. To the appeals of the men, he replied, "Gentlemen, it is impossible. I am worn out. I am not fit for the service, and cannot go."

That seemed to end the matter, but the spokesman of the group rose up, shook his head disparagingly, and said, "Well, I don't know what the neighbors will say." That struck home. "Oh, well," said Webster, "if it is the neighbors, I will go." And he went.

Commenting on this decision of Webster, Woodrow Wilson, in a notable address on Robert E. Lee, said, "There came to his mind the vision of some little group of old men in that village where he had lived as a boy whose comments he could surmise, and that was the particular condemnation he could not face."

Thomas Jefferson once said, "Love your neighbor as yourself and your country more than yourself."   *The Uplift*

YOU CAN WIN

Success isn't an overnight affair. Hidden talents may go undiscovered — unused — for years. Then something happens, and folks say that the successful one is "lucky".

Dr. Frank Crane was starved out of the ministry and forced to make a living in some other way. He did. He earned $1,000 a day as an inspirational essayist.

Jack Benny was a fiddler. Fred Allen was a librarian. Nelson Eddy presided at a telephone switchboard.

THE ORIGIN OF PAPER

It was a humble wasp which first gave the world paper. For centuries primitive man had carved hieroglyphics on stone, while following generations "wrote" on metal slabs, clay tablets, wax, and animal skins. Then along came the paper wasp, which chews vegetable fiber to pulp to form its nest. Ts'ai Lun, a Chinese minister, studied the habits of the wasp and in 105 A.D. successfully produced the first paper from bark and old linen. Unfortunately, the Chinese kept their secret for hundreds of years, and it was not until the 12th century that the news reached Europe.

SCHOOL DAYS OF OUR PRESIDENTS

It's a well-known fact that Abraham Lincoln had little schooling, and that Ulysses Grant and Dwight D. Eisenhower graduated from West Point, but are you familiar with the educational backgrounds of some of the other American Presidents? For instance:

Andrew Johnson never attended school, even for a day, and, when he married, his wife taught him to read and write. On the other hand, two of our Presidents have served as college presidents — Woodrow Wilson and Dwight Eisenhower. John Adams taught school for several years in Worcester, Massachusetts, in order to earn money to study law.

One future President was a playboy while in college. In his junior year, when he stood at the foot of the class, his friends persuaded him to reform. For three months he rose at 4 A. M. and retired at midnight, with the result that he graduated third in his class at Bowdoin. This was Franklin Pierce.

Strange as it seems, "Silent Cal" Coolidge was selected to deliver the humorous oration at a Class Day at Amherst. When Millard Fillmore fell in love with a village school-teacher, he admired her scholarly talents so much that he went to work and improved the limitations of his own sketchy schooling. James Madison had such a zeal for scholarship while in college that he nearly wrecked his health by sleeping only three hours out of the twenty-four to have more time for studying.

Three Presidents claimed William and Mary College as their alma mater — Thomas Jefferson, James Monroe, and John Tyler. One young man who later became President was expelled from college because of indifference and low grades. Later, when he made a successful plea for readmission, he was so changed in attitude that he was able to finish his college career as first in his class. This was James Buchanan.

William Henry Harrison, while studying to be a doctor, felt the call of patriotic duty and left college to fight the Indians.   *Erma Reynolds in Sunshine Magazine*

LIFE'S VALUES

Few men experience the complete solitude that became the lot of the late Admiral Richard E. Byrd, the famed explorer, on one of his trips into the frozen wastes of the Antarctic, and about which he wrote in his book, *Alone*. Trapped on a desolate barrier without the companionship of man or beast, and forced to remain there for a long time fighting cold, disease, and hunger, he had plenty of opportunities to reflect upon the meaning of life.

"My life became largely a life of the mind," he recounts. "Thinking things out alone on the barrier, I became better able to tell what in the world was wheat and what was chaff. I learned what philosophers have long insisted, that a man can live profoundly without masses of things. My definition of success itself changed. I came to believe that man's primary objective should be to seek a fair measure of harmony within himself and his family circle. Thus he achieves peace.

"I was conscious only of a mind utterly at peace, and yet I felt more alive than at any other time in my life. I saw my whole life pass in review. I realized how wrong my sense of values had been, and how I had failed to see that the simple, homely, unpretentious things of life are the most important. I thought of all I would do when I got home; and a thousand matters, which had never been more than casual, now became attractive and important." *Sunshine Magazine*

ARE YOU ILL?

In the French Chamber of Deputies, a young Deputy, who had been a veterinarian before going into politics, was in a debate.

"Is it true, my good man," said his opponent, "that you are actually a veterinarian?"

"It is, sir," said the young Deputy. "Are you ill?"

WHISTLER'S MODEL

An artist, having decided to paint the portrait of a woman, was searching for a model with a wistful expression. For days he interviewed prospects, but none seemed satisfactory. Discouraged, he gave up his interviews and began to walk the streets of London in search of a chance passerby whom he might persuade to be his model.

Weary, he returned to his studio and sat dejectedly before his ready canvas and easel. Suddenly the door opened, and a slender gray-haired woman softly entered the room. The artist looked up, smiled at her, and then began to gaze at her in wonder, as if he had never really seen her before. For years she had been one of his closest companions, but somehow he had never seen her just like this. She was the very type for whom he had been searching in vain! Perhaps she would be his model!

"Mother!" he exclaimed leaping to his feet. "Please sit in that chair!"

Although she protested, she laughingly obeyed him, confident that her son would soon discover that he had made a mistake in thinking that she could be his model.

Now the artist enthusiastically gave his instructions. "Please, Mother, look to this side. There, there! Now hold that position, please — just as you are."

Thus it was that James A. McNeill Whistler discovered in his own mother the model for his famous painting, *The Artist's Mother,* or *Whistler's Mother,* as it is generally called today. Whistler himself called it *Gray and Black,* for these were the only colors he used in the painting. Of all his works — and he produced many outstanding paintings — this is regarded as his masterpiece.   *Sunshine Magazine*

WHEN CIVILIZATIONS DIE

I do not think the greatest threat to our future is from bombs, or guided missiles. I don't think our civilization will die that way. I think it will die when we no longer care; when the spiritual forces that make us wish to be right and noble die in the hearts of men. Nineteen notable civilizations have died from within, and not been conquered from without. It happened slowly, in the quiet and dark, when no one was aware.   *Laurence K. Gould*

THE MAN WHO STRIVES

It is not the critic who counts — not the man who points out how the strong man stumbled, or where the doer of deeds could have done better. The credit belongs to the man who is actually in the arena; whose face is marred by dust and sweat and blood; who strives valiantly; who errs, and who comes short again and again. It is he who knows the great enthusiasm, the great devotions, and spends himself in a worthy cause; who at best knows in the end the triumphs of high achievement; and who, at the worst, if he fails, at least fails while daring greatly so that his place shall never be with those cold and timid souls who know neither defeat nor victory.   *Theodore Roosevelt*

THE MEANING OF CHRISTMAS

A little boy stood before the picture of his absent father, and then turned to his mother and wistfully said, "I wish Father would step out of the picture!"

This litle boy expressed the deepest yearning of the human heart. We who have gazed upon the pictures of God in nature are grateful, but not satisfied. We want our Father to step out of the impersonal picture and meet us as a Person. "The Impersonal laid no hold on my heart," says Tulsi Das, the great poet of India. It never does, for the human heart is personal and wants a personal response.

"Why won't principles do? Why do we need a personal God?" someone asks. Well, suppose you go to a child crying for its mother, and say, "Don't cry, little child; I'm giving to you the principle of motherhood." Would the tears dry and the face light up? Hardly. The child would brush aside your principle of motherhood and cry for its mother. We all want not a principle nor a picture, but a Person.

The Father has stepped out of the picture! The Word has become flesh! That is the meaning of Christmas.

E. Stanley Jones in Sunshine Magazine

COURAGE AND SACRIFICE

One stormy day a coast guard was ordered to the rescue of a liner wrecked off the coast of New England. An old and tried seaman was in charge, but the members of the crew were for the most part young, untested men. When one of them comprehended the situation, he turned white-faced to the captain and said, "Sir, the wind is off-shore, the tide is running out. We can go out, but against this wind and tide we cannot come back."

"We don't have to come back," replied the captain.

HE WHO KNOWS...

He who knows not and knows
not he knows not,
he is a fool — shun him;

He who knows not and knows he knows
　　not,
　　he is simple — teach him;
He who knows and knows not he knows,
　　he is asleep — wake him;
He who knows and knows he knows,
　　he is wise — follow him!

Arabic Apothegm

JAMES WALKER

Former Mayor Jimmy Walker of New York City was sounding off against a certain official in a newspaper interview.

"Then you'd say he's a total loss," asked the reporter.

"Oh, no," replied Mayor Walker. "He's not that good."

WINSTON CHURCHILL

Vic Oliver, an English comic, for a while happened to be Churchill's son-in-law. One day Oliver asked Churchill, "Who do you think was the greatest statesman in World War II?"

"Mussolini," Churchill glowered. "He had the courage to shoot his son-in-law."

ROSSINI

The opera composer, Rossini, was invited to dinner by a host who served very small portions. Rossini was still hungry at the meal's end.

"I do hope you'll do us the honor of dining here again," said the host.

Rossini replied, "Certainly, let's start now."

GEORGE BERNARD SHAW

One night George Bernard Shaw was discussing a subject dear to the heart of a woman in the lecture-hall audience.

Suddenly she stood up and said, "If you were my husband I'd poison you."

"Madame, if I were your husband," roared Shaw, "I'd *take* poison!"

SELF-RELIANT

Black is black, and not gray. The Constitution of the United States is the bedrock anchorage of our free society. Mankind is not admirable unless self-reliant. There can be no genuine strength in a welfare state. Government is dangerous — now and eternally.   *Barry Goldwater*

FREEDOM

If a nation wants prosperity more than freedom, wealth more than dignity, pleasure more than strength, brilliance more than character; if it considers that all the creative sacrifices have been endured by its ancestors; if it forgets that the individual holds his freedom as a trust for the nation, and the nation exists in service to humanity, individual freedom will be short-lived, and so will the free nation.

Dorothy Thompson

A SHORT SPEECH

It is said that airplane pioneers Wilbur and Orville Wright, a taciturn duo, hated to make speeches. Once, at a luncheon, they were scheduled to speak before a group of eminent inventors. The toastmaster called on Wilbur.

"There must be some mistake," stammered Wilbur. "Orville is the one who does the talking."

Then the toastmaster turned to Orville, who stood up and said, "Wilbur has just made the speech!"

A GENIUS

A young man once submitted a poem to William Dean Howells. "I think it is a magnificent poem," was the verdict.

"Did you compose it unaided?" "Yes, sir," said the young man, firmly. "I wrote every line of it out of my own head." Mr. Howells rose, and said: "Then, Lord Byron, I am very glad to meet you. I was under the impression that you had died a good many years ago!"

AND YOU THINK YOU HAVE IT TOUGH!

Following is a list of rules for teachers posted by a principal in the City of New York in 1872:

1. Teachers each day will clean lamps, clean chimneys, and trim wicks.

2. Each teacher will bring a bucket of water and a scuttle of coal for the day's session.

3. Make your pens carefully. You may whittle nibs to the individual tastes of the pupils.

4. Men teachers may take one evening each week for courting purposes, or two evenings a week if they go to church regularly.

5. After ten hours in school, the teachers should spend the remaining time reading the Bible or other good books.

6. Women teachers who marry, or engage in unseemly conduct, will be dismissed.

7. Every teacher should lay aside from each pay a goodly sum of his earnings for his benefit during his declining years, so that he will not become a burden on society.

8. Any teacher who smokes, uses liquor in any form, frequents pool or public halls, or gets shaved in a barber shop will give good reason to suspect his worth, intentions, integrity, and honesty.

9. The teacher who performs his labors faithfully and without fault for five years will be given an increase of twenty-five cents per week in his pay, providing the Board of Education approves.

Mrs. Nell Ferry, Brooklyn 17, N. Y., in Sunshine Magazine

CHAPTER V

INTERESTING IDEAS

TROUBLE

"I cannot prevent the birds of sorrow from passing over my head, but I can keep them from building a nest in my hair."   *Chinese Proverb*

FORMULA FOR FAILURE

I cannot give you the formula for success, but I can give you the formula for failure — which is: Try to please everybody.   *Herbert Bayard Swope*

THE TEST OF SCIENCE

The final test of science is not whether its accomplishments add to our comfort, knowledge, and power, but whether it adds to our dignity as men, our sense of truth and beauty. It is a test science cannot pass alone and unaided.
David Sarnoff

WEALTH

You may not have saved a lot of money in your life, but if you have saved a lot of heartaches for other folks, you are a pretty rich man.   *Seth Parker*

BIG SHOTS

Big shots are only little shots who keep shooting.
Christopher Morley

GRATITUDE

Two kinds of gratitude: The sudden kind we feel for what we take; the larger kind we feel for what we give.
E. A. Robinson

PERFECTION

There have been a few moments when I have known complete satisfaction, but only a few. I have rarely been free from the disturbing realization that my playing might have been better. *Jan Ignace Paderewski*

OPPRESSION AND YOUR BROTHER

Man never fastened one end of a chain around the neck of his brother, that God did not fasten the other end around the neck of the oppressor. *Lamartine*

SIMPLICITY

Be sincere. Be simple in words, manners and gestures. Amuse as well as instruct. If you can make a man laugh, you can make him think and make him like and believe you.
Alfred E. Smith

A BEGINNING

Fear not that Thy life shall come to an end, but rather fear that it shall never have a beginning.
Cardinal Newman

YOUR RESOURCES

Few men during their lifetime come anywhere near exhausting the resources dwelling within them. There are deep wells of strength that are never used.
Richard E. Byrd

GREAT MEN

The doctrine of human equality reposes on this: that there is no man really clever who has not found that he is stupid. There is no big man who has not felt small. Some men never feel small; but these are the few men who are.

Gilbert K. Chesterton

HOW MUCH ARE YOU WORTH

If you want to know how rich you really are, find out what would be left of you tomorrow if you should lose every dollar you own tonight.   *Wm. J. H. Boetcker*

INSECURITY

It's an old adage that the way to be safe is never to be secure. . . . Each of us requires the spur of insecurity to force us to do our best.   *Dr. Harold W. Dodds*

BOTH BRAIN AND HEART

In making our decisions, we must use the brains that God has given us. But we must also use our hearts which He also gave us.   *Fulton Oursler*

THE FAMILY

Woman knows what Man has too long forgotten, that the ultimate economic and spiritual unit of any civilization is still the family.   *Claire Booth Luce*

REWARD

There never was a person who did anything worth doing who did not receive more than he gave.

Henry Ward Beecher

WHAT ARE YOU LOOKING FOR

Many of us are like the little boy we met trudging along a country road with a catrifle over his shoulders. "What are you hunting, buddy?" we asked. "Dunno, sir, I ain't seen it yet."

R. Lee Sharpe

SYMPATHY

One of the finest and truest definitions of sympathy is, "Sympathy is your pain in my heart."

Halford E. Luccock

HE DID IT

Somebody said that it couldn't be done,
But he with a chuckle replied
That "Maybe it couldn't" but he would be one
Who wouldn't say so till he'd tried.
So he buckled right in with the trace of a grin
On his face. If he worried, he hid it.
He started to sing as he tackled the thing
That couldn't be done. And he did it.
Somebody scoffed, "Oh, you'll never do that,
At least no one ever has done it."
But he took off his coat and took off his hat
And the first thing he knew he'd begun it.
With the lift of his chin and a bit of a grin,
If any doubt rose he forbid it.
He started to sing as he tackled the thing
That couldn't be done, and he did it.
There are thousands to tell you it cannot be done,
There are thousands to prophesy failure;
There are thousands to point out to you, one by one,
The dangers that want to assail you.
But just buckle right in with a bit of a grin,
Then take off your coat and go to it.
Just start in to sing as you tackle the thing
That cannot be done, and you'll do it.

Author Unknown

YOUTH AND DISTINCTION

Not all men wait for old age to achieve distinction.

Galileo was only eighteen when he watched a lamp swinging in the cathedral at Pisa and conceived the principle of the pendulum clock.

Tennyson wrote his first volume at eighteen.

Lafayette was general of the French army at twenty.

Byron, who wrote *The Prisoner of Chillon* and many other poems, was dead at 37.

Rafael, whose paintings hang in the great galleries of the world, also died at 37.

Gladstone was in Parliament before he was twenty-two and was head of the British Treasury at twenty-four.

Victor Hugo wrote *The Hunchback of Notre Dame* at twenty-nine, but he was sixty before he wrote the great *Les Miserables*.

GENIUS COULD STILL LEARN

Michael Angelo, one of the greatest sculptors and painters of all time, had grown aged and blind. One day he groped his way into the Vatican gallery. With his face upturned, his hands felt the graceful lines of the sculptured torso of Phidias. Someone lingering near heard him say, "Great is this marble; greater still the hand that carved it; greatest of all, the God who fashioned the sculptor. I still learn! I still learn!" And so the blind sculptor who had painted the great fresco of *The Last Judgment* in the Sistine Chapel, and had carved the famous statue of *David*, could walk in darkness from the gallery knowing that he had "seen" perfect beauty. He could still learn.

PROGRESS

Every age has believed itself the last age of human achievement and every age has been wrong. Throughout the history of invention and discovery wise men have declared that we were at last straining the laws of nature when we were only straining our imaginations.

Charles Franklin Kettering

THE BEAT GENERATION

Precisely for what motives educators and publicists are pulling my leg by giving a new name to an old malady that we once cured with sulphur and molasses is difficult for me to understand. Historically, the Beat Generation is the bunk, and I know it and they should. Since the days of Cain and Abel, kids have been feeling sorry for themselves, and acting like goofs as a consequence, and blaming everyone else. . .
Earl Schenck Miers

THE HEARTS OF SMALL CHILDREN

The hearts of small children are delicate organs. A cruel beginning in this world can twist them into curious shapes . . . hard and pitted as the seed of a peach. . . . Or again, the heart . . . may fester and swell until it is . . . easily chafed and hurt by the most ordinary things.   *Carson McCullers*

HIGHER AND HIGHER

Man can never come to his ideal standard. It is the nature of the immortal spirit to raise that standard higher and higher as it goes from strength to strength, still upward and onward. Accordingly, the wisest and greatest are ever the most modest.   *Margaret Fuller*

THE WAY IT ALL STARTED

Back in 1776, James Watt advertised his newly invented steam engine in terms that miners would understand — horsepower. A horse walked 330 feet in one minute to hoist a 100-pound pail of coal, hence one horsepower equalled 33,000 foot pounds. It still does, too.

MY LITTLE VINE

Once I planted a vine beside a trellis. How carefully I tended the little sprout, watering it and teaching the tendrils to twine about the slats. Warmed by the strong sun, and nourished by the refreshing rain, the vine grew, and little by little climbed halfway up the trellis. In a little while it began to provide shade, and become a thing of beauty.

But one dark night a storm came. The wind blew furiously, and the rain fell in torrents. The next morning the little vine was lying on the ground, half submerged in muddy water.

I stooped down and tenderly lifted the fallen vine out of the mire, and twined it carefully about the trellis again. In places I fastened its tendrils to the slats with pieces of soft string. Then I watched it grow day by day, and observed with pleasure that the vine I had lifted up was taking a fresh hold.

Am I ever as considerate of my fellowmen — the men and women who suffer, and weep, and waver, and fall — as I was of that little vine, that knew neither pain nor pleasure? Am I as eager to lift up my brother man who has fallen low? Let us give men and women, with undying souls, as fair a chance to begin life over as we would an insignificant plant.

Author Unknown

GREAT DREAMS

We grow great by dreams. All big men are dreamers. They see things in the soft haze of a spring day or in the red fire of a long winter's evening. Some of us let these great dreams die, but others nourish and protect them; nurse them through bad days till they bring them to the sunshine and light which comes always to those who hope that their dreams will come true.   *Woodrow Wilson*

THIS IS MY COUNTRY

God grant that not only the love of liberty but a thorough knowledge of the rights of man may pervade all the nations of the earth, so that a philosopher may set his foot anywhere on its surface and say, "This is my country".

Benjamin Franklin

TRAVEL ABROAD

Though we travel the world over to find the beautiful, we must carry it with us or we find it not.

Ralph W. Emerson

DO YOUR PART

The woods would be silent
If no birds sang there
Except those that sang best.

John J. Audubon

LOVE YOUR ENEMIES

There is such a destructive action in the soul of a man who allows himself to hate another. Hate is a poison which brings about the degeneration of personality.

This story was told of General Robert E. Lee: Hearing General Lee speak in the highest terms to President Davis about a certain officer, another officer, greatly astonished, said to him, "General, do you not know that the man of whom you speak so highly to the President is one of your bitterest enemies, and misses no opportunity to malign you?"

"Yes," replied General Lee, "but the President asked my opinion of him; he did not ask for his opinion of me."

THE GREATEST ASSET

The greatest asset of any nation is the spirit of its people, and the greatest danger than can menace any nation is the breakdown of that spirit — the will to win and the courage to work.

George B. Cortelyou, Former Secretary of the Treasury

WRINKLES

If wrinkles must be written upon our brows, let them not be written upon the heart. The spirit should not grow old.

James A. Garfield

HOW EVIL TRIUMPHS

All that is necessary
For the triumph of evil
Is that good men do nothing.

Edmund Burke

CONSCIENCE

If you can remember the days when most persons had a conscience, you are getting old.

RANDOM THOUGHTS

Many people owe the grandeur of their lives to their tremendous difficulties.

Manners are the shadows of virtues, the momentary display of those qualities which our fellow creatures love and respect.   *Sydney Smith*

Working is more than a way of earning a livelihood; it is a way of keeping one's self-respect.

Those who are out to borrow trouble will find that they have an excellent credit rating.

Money won't buy friends, but it will get you a higher grade of enemies.

AN AMERICAN

An American is a guy who sips Brazilian coffee from an English cup while sitting on Danish furniture after coming home in his German car from an Italian movie — and then writes his Congressman with a Japanese ball point pen, demanding that he do something about all the gold that's leaving the country.   *Harry Lieberman*

WE'RE GETTING FASTER AND FASTER

In view of curent developments in rapid trans-oceanic travel, it is interesting to look back at some non-stop trans-Atlantic journeys that give high lights to the history of travel:

Columbus sailed from Palos, Spain, August 3, 1492; arrived at San Salvador, October 12; time elapsed, 69 days.

Pilgrim Fathers sailed from Plymouth, England, September 6, 1620; arrived at Cape Cod, November 19; time elapsed 74 days.

"Dreadnaught," Yankee clipper ship, sailed from New York, June 10, 1859; arrived Cape Clear, Ireland, on June 27; time, 17 days.

"Savannah," first steamship to cross the Atlantic from Savannah, Georgia, to Liverpool, leaving Savannah, May 24, 1818, crossing in 27 days.

"Great Eastern," famous early steamship, sailed from Needles, off Southampton, England, June 17, 1860; arrived New York, June 28; time elapsed, 11 days.

"Mauretania," sailed from New York to Cherbourg, September, 1924; time elapsed, 5 days, 1 hour and 40 minutes.

"Zeppelin Dirigible" (later "Los Angeles") sailed from Friedrichshafen, Germany, October 12, 1924; arrived Lakehurst, New Jersey, October 15; time elapsed, 81 hours, 17 minutes.

British Biplane took off at St. Johns, Newf., June 14, 1919; arrived Clifden, Ireland, June 15; time elapsed, 16 hours and 12 minutes.

Lindbergh's crossing from New York to Paris, in "The Spirit of St. Louis," in May, 1927; time elapsed, 33 hours, 29½ minutes.

For the most recent record of a trans-oceanic crossing consult the daily newspapers, as new records for speed are being made almost continually.

THE POWER OF GOD

Religion holds the solution to all problems of human relationship, whether they are between parents and children or nation and nation. Sooner or later, man has always had to decide whether he worships his own power or the power of God. When threats force him to look at the limitations of his human power, he's often ready to seek his spiritual one. What we need is patience and awe of God's plan in human history!   *Arnold Toynbee*

A MORE GLORIOUS EDIFICE THAN GREECE OR ROME

In his matchless eulogy on General Washington in 1832, Daniel Webster closed with these words:

"Other misfortunes may be borne, or their effects overcome. If disastrous war should sweep our commerce from the ocean, another generation might renew it; if it exhaust our treasury, future industry may replenish it; if it desolate and lay waste our fields, still, under new cultivation, they will grow green again, and ripen to future harvests.

"It were but a trifle even if the walls of yonder Capitol were to crumble, if its lofty pillars should fall, and its gorgeous decorations be all covered by the dust of the valley. All these may be rebuilt.

"But who shall reconstruct the fabric of demolished government?

"Who shall rear again the well-proportioned columns of constitutional liberty?

"Who shall frame together the skillful architecture which unites national sovereignty with State rights, individual security, and public prosperity?

"No, if these columns fall, they will be raised not again. Like the Coliseum and the Parthenon, they will be destined to a mournful and melancholy immortality. Bitterer tears, however, will flow over them than were ever shed over the monuments of Roman or Grecian art; for they will be the monuments of a more glorious edifice than Greece or Rome ever saw, the edifice of constitutional American liberty."

AMERICA

America is not anything if it consists of each of us. It is something if it consists of all of us; and it can consist of all of us only as our spirits are banded together in a common enterprise. That common enterprise is the enterprise of liberty and justice and right.   *Woodrow Wilson*

GREATNESS

We cannot all be great, but we can always attach ourselves to something that is great.   *Harry Emerson Fosdick*

FIGURES ARE FUNNY

Figures sometimes are funny things. For example, take the number 142857. Multiply it with any number from one to six, and you will get the same figures in the same order, but beginning at a different point.

After you have proved that, then multiply the original number by 7, and see what happens.

TWO LOVES

There are two loves from which all good and truth come: Love to the Lord and love to the neighbor. And there are two loves from which all evils and falsities come: the love of self and the love of the world.   *Emanuel Swedenborg*

OUR LIFE

Not one of us knows what effect his life produces, and what he gives to others; that is hidden from us and must remain so, though we are often allowed to see some little fraction of it, so that we may not lose courage.   *Albert Schweitzer*

LIFE

A man can fail many times, but he isn't a failure in life until he begins to blame somebody else.

Life is a grindstone, and whether it grinds a man down or polishes him up depends on the stuff he's made of.

Josh Billings

THE AMERICAN IDEAL

The American ideal is not that every man shall be on a level with every other, but that every one shall have liberty without hindrance to be what God made him.

York Trade Compositor

CURIOUS FACTS

If you are interested in geography, the following facts will give you something to think about:

The city of Montreal, Canada, lies west of that part of the Pacific Ocean which touches Chile.

The Gulf of California does not touch the State of California at any point.

The city of Reno, Nevada, lies 100 miles west of Los Angeles, California.

Rome, Italy, lies north of the southern shore of Lake Erie.

One travels south from Detroit, Michigan, to reach Windsor, Ontario, Canada.

Berlin, Germany, lies north of Saskatoon, Saskatchewan, Canada.

The Chatham Blanketeer

VACATION LAMENT

Little Bankroll, ere we part, let me press you to my heart. All the year I've clung to you; I've been faithful, you've been true. Little bankroll, in a day, you and I will start away to a good vacation spot. I'll come back, but you will not!

Sunshine Magazine

IDEAS

A shirt waving on a clothes line was the beginning of a great balloon, forerunner of the Zeppelin.

A spider web strung across a garden path was the inspiration for the suspension bridge.

A teakettle singing on the stove suggested the steam engine.

A lantern swinging in a tower gate gave rise to the pendulum.

An apple falling from a tree was the cause of discovering the law of gravity. *The War Cry*

THE PASSING SCENE

Thomas Mann, the German novelist, wrote: "What I value most is transitoriness." He went on to say that the passage of time is not sad, but the very soul of existence. It imparts value, dignity and interest. It prompts us to feel and answer the newness of every day that dawns.

When we cease peering backward into the mists of our past, and craning forward into the fog that shrouds the future, and concentrate upon doing what lies clearly at hand, then we are making the best and happiest use of our time.

We may suffer setbacks that seem to steal our time irretrievably. So Thucydides might have thought when, for losing a battle, he was exiled from Athens in 424 B. C. Instead, he spent the twenty years in banishment travelling from place to place gathering facts which he used in writing his immortal histories.

To have time for everything we wish to do we need to measure what we spent our time on in terms of its value in happiness and achievement.

Time moves on with the deliberation of universal processes that can afford to be slow because they have eternity for completion. As for us, we wake up in the morning and our purse is magically filled with twenty-four hours. We need to seek by all means the best ways in which we may make the most of our allowance.

Royal Bank of Canada Monthly Letter

ODD MOMENTS

Odd moments, like little things, add up quickly. When we count the blank spaces in our time we are likely to be embarrassed. Some are unavoidable, but many are the outcome of unpreparedness. Most of us, if caught in a traffic jam, for example, fret and fume. Noel Coward took a piece of paper from his pocket and wrote his popular song, "I'll See You Again."

To be prepared with little bits of things to do is to make sure of filling in the gaps, thus using all the time we have. It is not wise to wait for long uninterrupted periods. John Erskine said that he started pressing the odd five minutes into use. In every five minutes he wrote a hundred words or so. The result was his best-selling novel, *Helen of Troy*. Einstein had a dull, routine job in Switzerland, with many idle moments. Instead of visiting other office-holders, he spent that spare time in developing the first of his papers on relativity. A salesman, kept waiting by a prospective customer, used the time to telephone other prospects making appointments.

We can watch for little chunks of time — when the train is late, or dinner is delayed, or a caller is unpunctual — and have a pocket book ready to read.

To be alive is to dream, to plan, to aspire and to act, and time must be apportioned between these as a man sees best for himself. As Sir John Lubbock wrote: "Do what you will, only do something."

The Royal Bank of Canada Monthly Letter

BUSINESS CHARACTER

What a business stands for will never be anything different from what its people stand for. The respect it is held in will be determined by the respect they command as individuals and as a team. Do they have, and do they keep on getting, the knowledge they require for the job they are called on to do? Do they have the needs of the public and the good of the country deeply at heart? Can they always be relied on? Will they walk the second mile? Are they ceaselessly driving for excellence — for high quality — for performance that will astonish people because it is so good? Do they base their decisions and actions on what they earnestly believe is right for the long run, rather than on considerations of temporary advantage?

Frederick R. Kappel, Chairman of the Board, American Telephone and Telegraph Company

Senator Kenneth B. Keating once said, "House Speaker Sam Rayburn is the only one of our national monuments that talks."

DEFINITIONS

Hobby: Voluntary work.
Spring cleaning: Rearranging the dust.
Listening: Silent flattery.

CRITICISM

If criticism had any real power to harm, the skunk would be extinct by now. *Fred Allen*

SHORT SERMONS

In this world it is not what we take up but what we give up, that makes us rich.

We must not judge of a man's merits by his great qualities, but by the use he makes of them. *Rochefoucauld*

Next to knowing when to seize an opportunity, the most important thing in life is to know when to forego an advantage. *Disraeli*

INDUSTRY AND GENIUS

In the ordinary business life, industry can do anything which genius can do, and very many things which it cannot.
Henry Ward Beecher

GOD IS AWAKE

Have courage for the great sorrows of life, and patience

for the small ones. And when you have accomplished your daily task, go to sleep in peace. God is awake.

Victor Hugo

MORE NOISE

It is with narrow-souled people as with narrow-necked bottles: the less they have in them, the more noise they make pouring it out.

Alexander Pope

THOUGHTS

No one is useless in this world who lightens the burden of another.

Charles Dickens

A ship in the harbor is safe, but that is not what ships are made for.

J. A. Shedd

Character is not made in a crisis — it is only exhibited.

Robert Freeman

ATTENTION, GARDENERS

An American once asked an English gardener how he had developed such a wonderful lawn. He replied, "Well, we rolls it and cuts it, and we rolls it and cuts it; and we does this for two or three hundred years — and we gets a lawn like this."

DON'T WORRY

Don't worry if your job is small and your rewards are few. Remember that the mighty oak was once a nut like you.

TO LEARN, BE QUIET

A wise old owl sat on an oak,
The more he saw, the less he spoke,
The less he spoke, the more he heard —
Why can't we be like that wise old bird?

A BETTER MAN

Until we solve the human equation called man and get him straightened out, we will never have a peaceful world. You've got to build a better man before you can build a better society. *Billy Graham*

A JUDGE'S ADVICE

Always we hear the plaintive cry of teen-agers, "What can we do? Where can we go?" The answer is, "Go home!"

Hang the storm windows. Paint the woodwork. Rake the leaves. Mow the lawn. Sweep the walk. Wash the car. Learn to cook. Scrub the floors. Repair the sink. Build a boat. Get a job.

Help your minister, priest, or rabbi, the Red Cross, the Salvation Army. Visit the sick, assist the poor, study your lessons. And when you are through, and not too tired, read a book.

Your parents do not owe you entertainment. Your city or village does not owe you recreational facilities. The world does not owe you a living. But you owe the world something. You owe it your time and energy and your talents, so that no one will be at war, or in poverty, or be sick or lonely.

In plain, simple words, grow up! Quit being a cry-baby. Get out of your dream world, and develop a backbone, and start acting like a man (or a woman).

You are supposed to be mature enough to accept some of the responsibility your parents have carried for you for years. They have nursed, protected, excused, and tolerated you, and have denied themselves needed comforts so that you might have every benefit. They have done this gladly, for you are their dearest treasure.

But now, you have no right to expect them to bow to every whim and fancy of yours just because selfish ego instead of common sense dominates your personality, thinking, and requests. In Heaven's name, grow up and go home!

OUR CHANGING MORES

An observer has an opinion that women shed fewer tears at weddings than were shed a decade ago. This may be a product of our changing economy. With the current rate charged by baby sitters, relatives and friends of a young couple have reasonable assurance that they are not going away forever and that relationships will remain amicable.

The Matador (Tex.) Tribune

LIFE

So much is pressing in on humans today that no one has time to stand still long enough to evaluate it. They gulp life and taste nothing. They eat life and have no savor.

Geraldine Farrar, former opera star, on her eightieth birthday.

ENCOURAGEMENT

Every morning the sun rises, every spring the flowers bloom, every night the Great Dipper is just where it is supposed to be, most parents love their children, 98 per cent of our youngsters are not delinquents, most promises are faithfully kept, and there is still far more love than hate in the world, in spite of all the television and newspaper headlines.

Pana (Ill.) News-Palladium

ENTERTAINMENT AT A MEETING

Write down your house number. Double it. Add five. Multiply by 50. Add your age (don't cheat!). Then add 365 and subtract 615. In the resultant number you will find your house number is at the left and your age will be to the right.

TRY IT ON AN AUDIENCE

Think of a number, then double it. Add 4 and multiply by 5. Add 12 and multiply by 10. Subtract 320. Strike off the last two ciphers and you will again have the original number.

WORTH REMEMBERING

If we cannot get all we want, we should be thankful we don't get all we deserve.

He is not only idle who does nothing, but he is idle who might be better employed.

Little minds are wounded by little things.

DEBATE

When a Southerner talks at length, it's a filibuster; but when liberals do it, it's a protracted debate.

U. S. Senator Clinton P. Anderson

WHEN LIFE BEGINS

While in a mellow mood the other evening we wrote to a college classmate and expressed the sobering thought that with a twenty-fifth reunion coming up, two-thirds of our lives lie behind us. Graduation marked the first period, reunion will close the next 25 years, and most of us will be lucky if we last out another similar period of time.

Our classmate's reaction was prompt and indignant. "Maybe you can substantiate this in terms of years," he wrote, "but from the standpoint of contribution potential I'd guess that each of us has five or ten times more of his life to live than he has lived up to now."

We pass on that thought, fellow middle-aged readers, as both an encouragement and a challenge.

The Milford (N. H.) Cabinet

HARDER TO SAY

They said they made this year's Federal return easier to fill out. What they didn't say was that they also made it harder to pay.   *The Chapel Hill (N. C.) Weekly*

A MYTHICAL CREATURE

So far we have found no one who believes that he is over-paid and underworked.   *Granite City (Ill.) Press-Record*

IT'S UP TO YOU

If wages were a matter of negotiation, we would all nego-tiate ourselves a million dollars a year. But it isn't that simple.

You produce something; it is sold. That selling price has to include the cost of the material you used; it has to include taxes to support your government; it has to include a small — a very small — amount needed to keep your company in business. The rest is your wage.

If you produce more, there is obviously more for you. If you produce less, there is, of course, less for you.

You decide your wage by your production. And you decide something more — the security of your job. The less you produce efficiently, the more it costs. The more it costs, the fewer people there are who will buy it. The fewer people who buy it, the less demand for your work — the less secure your job.

Prices and wages and job security are a question of efficient production. And that is your responsibility.

Warner and Swasey, Cleveland

WHAT YOU GIVE AWAY

What you save, you leave behind; what you spend, you have for awhile, but what you give away, you take with you.

DO IT NOW

You cannot do a kindness too soon, for you never know how soon it will be too late.   *Ralph W. Emerson*

A SCHOOL TEACHER DISCUSSES SOCIALISM

A high school teacher in Yonkers, N. Y., recently made the following report as to the possible application of socialism in the schools:

As a teacher in the public schools, I find that the socialist-communist idea of taking "from each according to his ability," and giving "to each according to his need," is now accepted without question by most of our pupils. In an effort to explain to them the fallacy in this theory, I sometimes use the following approach.

When one of the brighter or harder-working pupils makes a grade of 95 on a test, I suggest that I take away 20 points and give them to a student who has made only 55 points on his test. Thus each would contribute according to his ability, and, since both would have a passing mark, they would share equally.

After I have juggled the grades of all the other pupils in this fashion, the result is usually a "common ownership" grade of between 75 and 80 — the minimum needed for passing, or for survival. Then I speculate with the pupils as to the probable results if I used this theory for grading papers.

First, the highly productive pupils — and they are always a minority in school as well as in life — would soon lose all incentive.

Second, the less productive pupils would, for a time, be relieved of the necessity of study. This system would continue until the high producers had sunk to the level of the low producers. At that point, in order for anyone to survive, the "authority" would have no alternative but to set up a system of compulsory labor and punishment against even the low producers.

Finally, I return the discussion to the ideas of freedom and enterprise — the market economy — where each person has freedom of choice, and is responsible for his own decisions and welfare. And most of my pupils then understand what I mean when I explain that socialism — even in a democracy — will eventually result in a living death for all except the "authorities" and a few of their favorite lackeys.

BRIEF THOUGHTS

The highest reward a man can receive for his toil is not what he gets for it, but what he becomes by it.

When you've made a fool of yourself, a real friend doesn't feel that you've done a permanent job.

The blossom cannot tell what becomes of its odor, and no man can tell what becomes of his influence and example, that roll away from him, and go beyond his ken on their perilous mission. *H. W. Beecher*

EMPTY HEAD

If a fellow has an empty stomach, it won't let him rest until he fills it. An empty head doesn't do the same.

LIBERTY

The real democratic American idea is not that every man shall be on a level with every other, but that everyone shall have liberty, without hindrances, to be what God made him.
Henry Ward Beecher

THE INDEPENDENT INVENTOR

The frozen food industry was pioneered by Clarence Birdseye, a biologist.

The Garand rifle was invented by John C. Gerand, a member of the New York National Guard.

Polaroid glass (antiglare) was invented by Edwin H. Land, a student.

Television: important developments were pioneered by an independent inventor, Philo T. Farnsworth.

Neoprene, first U. S. synthetic rubber, was developed from suggestions by Father Julius Nieuwland, a college professor.

The basic radio vacuum tube was invented by a struggling inventor, Lee De Forest.

IDEAS

Character is the capacity to conduct one's self with restraint in times of prosperity and with courage and tenacity when things do not go well.   *James V. Forrestal*

You don't have to go places if you are happy where you are.

The smallest good deed is better than the grandest good intention.

Fortify yourself with contentment, for this is an impregnable fortress.

It shouldn't be necessary to blow out the other person's light to let yours shine.

Only when we walk in the dark do we see the stars.

The best day — today.

The biggest ignoramus — the boy who will not go to school.

The most agreeable companion — one who would not have you any different from what you are.

The greatest deceiver — one who deceives himself.

The greatest comfort — the knowledge that you have done your work well.

The greatest mistake — giving up.

The three expensive indulgences — self-pity, hate and anger.

The greatest stumbling block — egotism.

The most ridiculous asset — pride.

The best teacher — one who makes you want to learn.

The meanest feeling — feeling bad at another's success.

The greatest happiness — helping others.

The greatest thing in all the world — LOVE.

TOO FAST FOR HIM

The four-year old was out for a walk with his father. He was finding it quite a problem to keep up with the grown-up strides.

"Am I walking too fast?" asked the father.

"No," panted the lad, "but I am!"

A PRICE TAG

There is a price tag on human liberty. That price is the willingness to assume the responsibilities of being free men. Payment of this price is a personal matter with each of us. To let others carry the responsibilities of freedom and the work and worry that accompany them — while we share only in the benefits — may be a very human impulse, but it is likely to be fatal.   *Eugene Holman*

QUOTATIONS FROM FAMOUS PEOPLE

A really successful politician should see only one side of a question.   *Lord Shawcross*

I am in agreement with Christ on many things.
Soviet Prime Minister Nikita S. Khrushchev

Every man has the right to a Saturday night bath.
Vice President Johnson

Modern man is not becoming sinless; he is just becoming lacking in a sense of sin.
The Church of England's Archbishop of York

If anyone has a new idea in this country, there are twice as many people who advocate putting a man with a red flag in front of it.   *Prince Philip, Queen Elizabeth's husband*

Getting angry about history is a sterile occupation, and in any case, it blinds those who indulge in it to events of the present.   *Prince Philip*

Being a judge is the best career in the world. One is never contradicted, one is never interrupted, and one always has the last word.   *Britain's Justice Vaisey*

Three-quarters of television is for halfwits. The boxing is all right.   *Conductor Sir Thomas Beecham*

Old age isn't so bad when you consider the alternative.
Maurice Chevalier

We are going to make the imperialists dance like fishes in a saucepan, even without war.   *Khrushchev*

I can see nothing objectionable in the total destruction of the earth, provided it is done, as seems likely, inadvertently.
Novelist Evelyn Waugh

CHAPTER VI

HUMOROUS STORIES AND ANECDOTES

NEXT QUESTION

Little Johnnie had to stand in the corner at school for putting mud in a little girl's mouth. His mother was horrified when she heard about it. "Why in the world," she wanted to know, "did you put mud in Margaret's mouth?"

"Well," said Johnnie, shrugging his shoulders, "it was open."

THE BIG ONE GOT AWAY

If a fisherman fibs to us,
Is his fib amphibious?

SHE GOT ALMOST EVERYTHING

Our little niece got four books, three handkerchiefs and the measles at her birthday party.

SIGN IN FRUIT STORE

Cantaloupe
Our choice 25 cents
Your choice 35 cents

IS THAT CLEAR

Football coach: "Football develops initiative and leadership. Now get in there and follow my instructions."

DO-IT-YOURSELF

The wife was guiding the middle-aged man, bent at the waist, into the doctor's office.

Receptionist: "Arthritis with complications?"

Wife: "No, do-it-yourself — with concrete blocks!"

FAIR EXCHANGE

A firemen's organization, conducting a ticket-selling campaign for the annual dance, featured this slogan: "You come to our dance and we'll go to your fire."

KEEP CHRISTMAS

Department store sign: Keep Christmas with you all year — use our monthly payment plan.

SAVED TOO MUCH

"I hear you've been having a hard time with that new car of yours. What's wrong?" asked a friend.

"Well, I bought a carburetor that saved 30 per cent on gas, a timer that saved 50 per cent on gas, and spark plugs that saved 30 per cent on gas, and after I drove 10 miles, the gas tank overflowed!"

A GOOSE

A certain schoolboy was asked to write an essay about a goose, and he wrote the following:

"The goose is a low heavy set bird, composed mostly of meat and feathers. His head sets on one end he sets on the other. He cannot sing much on account of the dampness in the moisture in which he lives. There ain't no space between his toes, and he carries a balloon in his stomach to keep from sinking.

"A goose has two legs on his running gear, but they came pretty near missing his body. Some geese when they get big are called ganders. Ganders don't have to set or hatch, but just loaf, eat, and go swimming. If I was a goose, I'd rather be a gander."

CORRECT

"Bobby," said the teacher, "tell me which month of the year has twenty-eight days in it."

Bobby had forgotten, but after a moment of deep thought he shouted, "They all have!"

PRETTY LOW

One day, while lecturing to his Shakespeare class, Harvard's famed George Lyman Kittredge accidentally stepped off the platform and fell to the floor. Scrambling to his feet, he remarked, "In 40 years of teaching, this is the first time I have ever descended to the level of my audience."

IT WASN'T EASY

Waitress: "How did you find your steak, sir?"

Hungry diner: "It was just luck. I happened to move a piece of parsley and there it was!"

NOW WE KNOW

An authority on the popular synthetic fiber, nylon, has generously supplied this enlightening explanation of its make-up:

Nylon, he says, is "a generic term for any long-chain synthetic polymeric amide which has recurring amide groups as an integral part of the main plymer chain, and which is capable of being formed into a filament in which the structural elements are oriented in the direction of the axis."

No wonder it's so expensive!

THE WRONG VERSE — CHECK IT

According to Mrs. Dean B. Howell of Forksville, Pa., a man who was staying at home during the past summer while his wife visited relatives, became concerned when he failed to receive his wife's weekly letter. He thought he would be smart and send her a quotation from the Bible that would surely bring a letter by the next mail. Not having a Bible handy, he depended on his memory and wrote: "My dear wife — Proverbs 25:24 — John."

His Biblical reference failed to have the desired effect, for he received no more letters from his wife. When she returned home, he asked why she had not written. Without a word, she pointed out his quotation. He glanced at it and exclaimed, "No wonder! I cited the wrong verse! It should have been Proverbs 25:25."

UNREASONABLE PERSON

"Look here, private, this man beside you on this fatigue detail is doing twice the work you are."

"I know, sarge. That's what I've been telling him for the last hour, but he won't slow down."

CORRECT ANSWER

It was the little girl's first day at school, and the teacher was making out her registration card.

"What is your father's name?" asked the teacher.

"Daddy," replied the child.

"Yes, I know, but what does your mother call him?"

"Oh, she doesn't call him anything — she likes him!"

SHREWD OBSERVER

The defense was ably represented by two dapper city attorneys who worked in shifts and put on quite an impressive show. In spite of all this, however, the lawyer for the plaintiff was very well satisfied with the way things were going when the court recessed for lunch, and he was therefore, shocked when his client insisted on getting another lawyer to assist.

"I'm doing all right," the lawyer remonstrated, "why do you want another lawyer?"

"Well," replied the plaintiff, "I've been watchin' them other lawyers, and when one of them is up speakin', the other one is sittin' there thinkin'. But when you're up speakin', there ain't nobody thinkin'!"

DON'T GO TOO FAR

First Rookie: "I feel like punching that top sarge in the nose again!"

Second Rookie: "What do you mean, again?"

First Rookie: "Well, I felt like it yesterday, too."

WE'VE HAD IT HAPPEN

Inquired the medical student of the well-known doctor, "Is it true, sir, that eating fish stimulates the brain?"

"Probably," replied the doctor. "But one thing is certain — going fishing stimulates the imagination."

SLOW IN ARRIVING

"How old did you say you were?" asked the doctor of his patient.

"I never mention my age," replied the young woman, "but as a matter of fact, I've just reached twenty-one."

"Indeed?" said the doctor; "what detained you?"

IT MAKES HIM HAPPY

A farmer was an incurable grumbler. One fall he had the best apple crop for miles around. One of his neighbors stopped by to congratulate him, and said, "Well, Hiram, you sure ought to be happy now. This is the finest crop of apples ever raised around these parts."

But the grumbler didn't even smile, as he growled, "Well, I s'pose they'll do — but where's the rotten ones for the hogs?"

WE DON'T BLAME HIM

An American tourist returning from Wales reports that whenever the through trains stop at Llanfechpwllgogerych, the conductor simply calls out: "If anybody's getting off here, this is it!"

EXPECTING TOO MUCH

It was to offset Jack Dempsey's reputation as a rough, tough hombre that Gene Tunney was built up as a gentleman boxer before their first battle for the world's championship. The campaign turned slightly sour when wise-crackers laughed at stories of Tunney reading Shakespeare.

An innocent young interviewer cornered Tunney one day for a story. "And have you ever written anything yourself, Mr. Tunney?"

Tunney reddened with anger. "No!" he thundered. "There are enough people sore at me because I can read. What do you suppose they would say if they thought I could write, too?"

FIGURES CAN'T LIE?

"Figures can't lie," said the instructor. "For instance, if one man can build a house in twelve days, twelve men can build it in one."

A puzzled student interrupted: "Then 288 will build it in one hour, 17,280 in one minute, and 1,036,800 in one second. I don't believe they could lay one brick in that time."

While the instructor was still gasping, the "ready reckoner" went on: "And again, if one ship can cross the Atlantic in six days, six ships can cross in one day. I can't believe that either."

SHAKESPEAREAN COMMERCIALS

If Shakespeare were alive today, writing for radio or television, we might have commercials reading something like this:

"Let me have about me men that are fat, sleek-headed men, and such as sleep o'nights with 'Sanka.' "

"Yon Cassius has a lean and hungry look. Me thinks he has not had his 'Wheaties' this morn."

"The quality of mercy is not strained; it falleth like the gentle rain from heaven upon the place beneath jt. Like gifts from Ye Olde Giftie Shoppe, 2032 West Hamilton Drive, it blesseth him who gives and him who takes."

Upward

YES AND NO

Said the gentleman to the youngster, "Son, how old are you?"

"Ten, sir," came the answer.

"Then you go to school, naturally."

"Well, yes and no," said the youngster cautiously.

"What do you mean — yes and no?"

"I go to school, but not naturally."

NOBODY HOME

An angry young man dashed into the electrician's shop. "Didn't I ask you yesterday morning to send a man to mend our doorbell?" he roared, "and did you not promise to send him around at once?"

"But we did, sir," broke in the manager. "I'm quite sure of it! Hi, Bill!" he called to one of his workmen. "Didn't you go around to Park Lodge yesterday to do that job?"

"Yes sir," replied Bill. "I rang the bell for over ten minutes, but I couldn't get no answer, so I guessed they must not be at home."

HARD JOB

"It's becoming increasingly difficult to reach the down-trodden masses in America," a Comrade wrote to his superior. "In the spring they're forever polishing their cars. In the summer they take vacations. In the fall they go to the world series and football games. And in the winter you can't get them away from their television sets. Please tell me how to let them know they are oppressed."

SHE TAUGHT HIM

A pupil was having trouble with punctuation, and was being taken to task by the teacher.

"Never mind, Sonny," said the visiting school-board president, consolingly, "it's foolish to bother about commas. They don't amount to much, anyway."

"Elizabeth Ann," said the teacher to a small girl in the class, "please write this sentence on the board: 'The president of the board says the teacher is misinformed.' Now," she continued, "put a comma after 'board,' and another after 'teacher!' "

BOTH SATISFIED

A man, applying for a job, wrote on his application that he left his last job because of illness.

"What, exactly, do you mean by illness?" asked the manager.

After some hemming and hawing, the applicant explained: "I got sick of the boss, and he got sick of me."

WE AGREE

Since the earth's surface is one-quarter land and three quarters water, it seems obvious that we are intended to spend three times longer fishing than we do mowing the lawn.

GOOD MEMORY

"You remember Jim Barrington?"
"Yes, I do, what's his name?"
"How should I know?"

PROMPT CUE

Whose memory does not include some marvelous fluff that took place in a school or church pageant?

A little lad forgot his lines in a Sunday School presentation.

His mother was in the front row to prompt him. She gestured and formed the words silently with her lips, but it did not help. Her son's memory was blank.

Finally she leaned forward and whispered the cue, "I am the light of the world."

The child beamed and with great feeling declaimed in a loud, clear voice: "My mother is the light of the world."

QUALIFIED

With the recruitment rush, an about-to-be soldier was being interviewed.

"Did you go to grammar school?" asked the sergeant.

The recruit drew himself up. "Yes, sir!" he stated. "I also completed high school, graduated *cum laude* from college and then completed four years at Harvard which granted me my doctorate."

The sergeant nodded amiably, reached for a rubber stamp and pressed it to the questionnaire. It read: "Literate."

OPTIMIST

A bridegroom making plans as to what he will do with his next pay check.

GOOD ANSWER

H. L. Mencken had a bad time pondering over what to do about the many controversial letters he received until he devised a fool-proof, final and courteous reply that seemed to cover every case adequately. It said:

Dear Sir:
You may be right.
Cordially,
H. L. Mencken.

HE KNEW THEM

"You pay a small deposit," said Harry to a prospective customer, "and make no payments for six months."

"Come on, Tony," said his wife, pulling her husband toward the door. "Somebody's told him about us!"

THEY ARE HARD TO FIND

"What we need," said the personnel manager, "is a man of vision, a man with drive, determination, fire, a man who never quits, a man who can inspire others, a man who can pull the Company's bowling team out of last place."

KEEP CALM

A man in a supermarket was pushing a cart which contained, among other things, a screaming baby.

As the man proceeded along the aisles, he kept repeating softly: "Keep calm, Albert," "Don't get excited, Albert," "Don't yell, Albert."

A lady watched with admiration and then said: "You are certainly to be commended for your patience in trying to quiet little Albert."

"Lady," he declared, "I'm Albert."

BE PATIENT

We note the arrival of an electric toothbrush, but no answer has yet been found to the drudgery of squeezing the toothpaste out of the tube.

COOPED UP

"Honest now," demanded the Texan, "don't you think Texas has it all over Alaska as a place to live?"

"Oh, Texas is a nice place, all right," conceded the Alaskan. "And I think I'm going to like it here — once I get over that cooped-up feeling."

PUZZLED PEASANT

Two peasants were watching a parade.

As the soldiers marched past, Ivan asked "Mischa, do men grow upward or downward?"

"Downward, of course," asserted Mischa.

"How do you know?"

"Because I once outgrew my overcoat and it became too short for me at the bottom."

"I think you are wrong, Mischa. I believe that men grow upward."

"Why do you say so?"

"Look at those soldiers marching. You will see that they are all even at the bottom, but uneven at the top."

HE KNOWS

Sign at a local used-car lot: "You think it's junk? Come in and price it!"

OUR GARAGE

It's stacked with piles of paper, and with bottles to return; with chicken wire and kindling, and with pots for planting ferns.

It's crammed with kiddies' playthings, and with sacks of mulch and lime, as well as chairs and things we hope to fix when we've got time.

And over in the corner there, and not a bit too wide, there's room, if we look very sharp, to drive our car inside!

Doings in Denton, Texas

WE KNOW

One housewife to another, over the back fence: "I got to thinking yesterday — you know how you do when the television set is broken . . ."

AVERAGE MAN

Wife: "Dear, what is meant by the expression, 'the average man'?"

Husband: "An average man, hon, is one who isn't as good as his wife thinks he is before she marries him, and not as bad as she thinks he is afterward."

IMPOSSIBLE

In a village election in Mississippi, one Republican vote was discovered before the tabulation had been completed. Election officials stopped to ponder this marvel, then decided to complete the count.

Soon another Republican vote turned up. "That settles it," said one of the officials. "That guy voted twice!"

THAT'S DIFFERENT

When you say that you've troubles as great as my own,

I'm forced to admit that it's true; but consider the fact that mine happen to me, while yours merely happen to you.

WE UNDERSTAND

They spent the evening dining. They danced, and then a show. She had no thought of the expense; the money — it did go!

They parted at the front door; she whispered with a sigh, "I'll be home tomorrow night." He answered, "So will I!"

HOW TIMES HAVE CHANGED

The Old Days: We were broke, so we lived on hamburger for a week.

Now: We lived on hamburger for a week, so we were broke.

YOU TELL 'EM LADY

Three ladies were having tea at the Waldorf. The first said: "My husband bought me some diamond bracelets. Then my skin broke out, and the doctor said I was allergic to diamonds. So we had to return them."

The second said that her husband had bought her a fur coat, which had to be returned because the doctor said she was allergic to furs.

The third fainted. When she was revived, she explained, "I'm allergic to hot air."

CORRECT

"Some plants," said the teacher, "have the prefix dog. For instance, there is the dogrose, the dogwood, the dog-violet. Who can name another plant prefixed by dog?"

"I can," shouted a little redhead from the back row. "Collie flower."

HE LEARNED THEM

"What did Mama's little boy learn in school today?" asked the doting mother.

Bill: "I learned two of the kids not to call me 'Mama's little boy.'"

HE KNEW

A father, buying a doll for his little girl for Christmas, was told by the saleslady: "Here's a lovely doll — you lay her down and she closes her eyes, just like a real little girl."

Said the sadly experienced father: "I guess, lady, you've never had a real little girl."

IS THAT CLEAR?

A little boy seated himself in a barber's chair and declared he wanted a haircut.

"How would you like it cut, son?" asked the barber.

"Like Grandpa's," he said.

"How's that?"

"Real short," said the boy, "with a hole in the top."

WE THINK ALIKE

An American staying in a London hotel was introduced to a man from Edinburgh who asked him, "An' what country do you belong tae?"

"The greatest country in the world!" replied the American.

"Mon! So dae I," replied Sandy, "but you dinna speak like a Scotsman."

ECONOMIST AND STATISTICIAN

An economist begins by knowing a very little about a great deal, and gradually gets to know less and less about more and more until he finally gets to know practically nothing about practically everything.

A statistician begins by knowing a very great deal about a very little, and gradually gets to know more and more about less and less, until he finally gets to know practically everything about nothing.

WHAT ARE YOU?

We've often wondered how waitresses could remember the various orders for different meals that they receive. Now we know, because while we were getting impatient at our table the other day, we called to the girl: "Waitress, have you forgotten me?"

She answered pertly, "Oh, no, sir. Indeed not. You're the stuffed tomato!"

THE WEEKEND

Monday — Recovery from last weekend.
Tuesday — Make arrangements for next weekend.
Wednesday — Lull between weekends.
Thursday — Get ready for weekend.
Friday — Leave for weekend.
Saturday and Sunday — Weekend.

IN OTHER WORDS

It is not always easy to say the right thing on the spur of the moment.

We can sympathize with the chap who met an old friend after many years.

"How is your wife?" he asked.

"She is in Heaven," replied the friend.

"Oh, I'm sorry," stammered the chap. Then he realized this was not the thing to say.

"I mean," he stammered, "I'm glad."

That seemed even worse so he blurted:

"Well, what I really mean is, I'm surprised."

THAT'S ALL

A lady visited a crystal gazer and was shocked to learn that her fee was twenty-five dollars, which, stated the seer "entitles you to ask me two questions."

"Isn't that a lot of money for only two questions?" demanded the lady.

"Yes, madam, it is," replied the fortune teller. "And now what is your second question?"

"Have I asked one?"

"Yes, and that's the second."

INTRODUCTIONS

Mr. Motley: That's quite an introduction. I have traveled a couple of hundred thousand miles this last year and have attended a couple of hundred meetings as President of the United States Chamber and I've had a lot of introductions. I can only remember two of them:

One chap, with conscious humor, said, "This man needs no introduction, just a conclusion."

The other fellow was an unconscious wit. He said, "I will not make a long, boring speech introducing Mr. Motley, he will —." *Arthur Motley*

THE SERGEANT WAS FRESH

The major who received a complaint about the issue of bread, snapped angrily, "If Napoleon had had that bread in Russia, he would have eaten it with the greatest pleasure."

"Yes, sir," spoke up the sergeant; "but it was fresh then."

TELL ME ABOUT HARRY

Rep. John Anderson of Illinois observes that many campaign speeches remind him of the story of a young man who proposed apologetically to the object of his affections.

"I don't have a lot of money, a yacht, and a convertible like Harry Smith, but I love you," the suitor said.

"And I think you're very sweet," the girl answered, "but tell me more about Harry."

FAR SIGHTED

Flying to Los Angeles from San Francisco the other day, a passenger noticed that the "Fasten Seat Belts" sign was kept alight during the entire journey, although the flight was a particularly smooth one. Just before landing, he asked the stewardess about it.

"Well," explained the girl, "up front there are seventeen University of California girls going to Los Angeles for the weekend. In back, there are twenty-five Coast Guard enlistees. What would you do?"

WHERE ARE THEY?

Teacher: "Where's your pencil, Alfred?"
Alfred: "Ain't got one, teacher."
Teacher: "How many times have I told you not to say that? Listen: I haven't got one, you haven't got one, we haven't got one, they haven't got one —"
Alfred: "Well, where are all the pencils?"

BAD FIX

Jones: "I'm in an awful fix!"
Smith: "What's the matter?"
Jones: "I lost my glasses, and I can't look for them till I find them!"

OF COURSE

The teacher was talking about the North-American Indians. She asked if anyone could tell what the leaders of the tribes were called.

"Chiefs," said a little girl.

"Correct," said the teacher. "Now, what were the women called?"

A smart little boy answered, "Mischiefs."

PRETTY FAST

An American army officer stationed in Australia decided to go on a kangaroo hunt. He climbed into his jeep and instructed his Negro driver to proceed to the plains in quest of a kangaroo. Soon they spotted one, and the driver drove the jeep in hot pursuit.

For some time they went at breakneck speed without gaining on the animal. Finally, the driver shouted to the officer, "Ain't no use chasin' that thing, suh!"

"Why not?" asked the officer.

"'Cause we's now doin' 65, and that critter ain't even put his front feet down yit!"

NOTHING BETTER COMING

Little Alice was helping her mother serve the dessert. She gave the first dish of pudding to her father, who offered it to the guest on his right. Returning with another dish and seeing that her father had none, she served him again. He in turn handed it on to his left.

When Mary came in with the third dish, she placed it in front of her father and said, "Daddy, you might as well keep this one. They're all alike."

IT WASN'T EASY

The little lad sat upon a fence looking up at the bright red apples that hung on the branches of a laden tree. Suddenly the farmer leaped from a bush and screamed, "Are you trying to steal my apples?"

"No, sir," replied the lad. "I'm trying not to."

VERY DIFFICULT

One of the most difficult instruments to play well is second fiddle.

IT CERTAINLY IS

An employer interviewing an applicant remarked, "You ask high wages for a man with no experience."

"Well," he replied, "it's so much harder to work when you don't know anything about it."

A LITTLE EXERCISE

Two women who were maneuvering their car into a tight parking space gave up after a valiant struggle when the driver shut off the motor and said to her companion: "This is close enough. We can walk to the curb from here."

THE SECRETARY'S JOB

Personnel Director: "What previous experience have you had and what work have you done?"

Pretty Job Candidate: "I was a secretary. All I had to do was to look like a girl, think like a man, act like a lady and work like a dog."

AND FOUR MORE PAYMENTS

The girl was thrilled when her boy friend brought her a beautifully wrapped Christmas gift. It contained some nice perfume and powder. The enclosed card read: "To Jane: With all my love, and most of my allowance."

IT MIGHT BE

Edward R. Murrow, director of the United States Information Agency, at a convention of radio and television news directors, told them they have heavy responsibilities. Illustrating a point, he recalled an early morning after the worst night of the London blitz in World War II.

"I had been driving around all night in an open car with

an old and cynical friend, wise in the ways of reporting," Murrow said. "When we got back to our typewriters, I confessed the obvious — that I didn't know how to write the piece.

" 'It's simple,' he said. 'Just sit down and write it as if it were your last story, because you know, it just might be.' "

INSECURE

Mother of small boy to child psychiatrist: "Well, I don't know whether or not he feels insecure, but everybody else in the neighborhood certainly does."

AND SOON

A young college student wrote home to his family:
"Dear Mom and Dad: I haven't heard from you in nearly a month. Please send a check so I'll know you're all right."

NEEDED A REST

A shoe salesman who had dragged out half his stock to a woman customer: "Mind if I rest a few minutes, lady? Your feet are killing me."

WE'VE SEEN OTHERS

After boasting of his prowess as a marksman, the hunter took aim on a lone duck overhead.

"Watch this," he commanded his listeners. He fired and the bird flew on.

"My friends," he said with awe, "you are now viewing a miracle. There flies a dead duck."

THE OLD DAYS

The final minutes of a Senate session were enlivened by the wit of Senator Dirksen in his farewell to his colleagues. In cautioning against haste, the eloquent senator turned to the days of the horse and buggy.

"When a young man came to court his lady love, he did not come in a Corvair, or a Galaxy, or a Cadillac," Dirksen said. "He came in an old buggy drawn by a horse and took his time; and when he got to the home of his lady love, he put the horse in the stable, and then was ushered into the parlor which was opened only one day a week. Then he would sit on one end of the horsehair sofa and she on the other. Then there would be that quiet agonizing hour after hour as they said exactly nothing.

"I remember on one occasion, after such an agonizing and excruciating loveliness, a young man blurted out, 'Matty, how's your maw — not that I give a hang, but just to make conversation?'"

INCOME TAX

Mortimer Caplin, who as commissioner of internal revenue is the nation's chief tax collector, gets lots of mail. One taxpayer wrote: "I have saved nearly three shopping bags of empty medicine bottles to substantiate my medical expenses. My husband says I'm crazy. Do you think I'm crazy?"

Another taxpayer, who had been informed by the revenue office that his federal tax return had failed to state specifically the nature of his business, replied:

"My principal occupation, in which I seem to spend most of my time is filling out government forms. I try to make cheese on the side."

IT WAS DIFFICULT

"Children," said the teacher, "be diligent and steadfast, and you will succeed. Take the case of George Washington. Do you remember my telling you of the great difficulty George Washington had to face?"

"Yes, ma'am," said a boy. "He couldn't tell a lie."

PURE WATER

A patient at a southern health resort visited one of the many medical springs on the resort grounds and asked an old caretaker he found if the spring water was pure.

"Yessuh!" said the old man. "Dis water sure am pure. It hab been scandalized by de bes' phrelologists in de lan', and dey say dat it contains seven per cent exide acid, eleben per cent cowbonic acid, an' de res' am pure hydrophobia."

FIRST THINGS FIRST

Announcer: "We have just received a flash of a catastrophe, the like of which has never been known to mankind. But first a word from our sponsor."

HE GOT PAID

A dentist in a small town had trouble obtaining payment on an overdue account. After thinking deeply about the matter, he decided to write the patient as follows:

"Dear Madam: Unless the denture I made for you is paid for without delay, I shall be obliged to insert the following advertisement in the newspaper: 'Excellent set of teeth for sale. They can be seen at any time at Mrs. Bartlett's, 129 Pinetree Road.'"

The dentist got his money the next morning.

Capper's Weekly

FAR-SIGHTED

A draftee on his way to training camp asked another draftee, "Do you happen to have a match?"

"Sure," was the second draftee's reply. "But I'm making sure not to give you any!"

"But why?" was the startled query from the first recruit.

"Well," said the second, "we'll get to talking, and if we get to talking, we'll wind up as buddies. And if we're buddies, we'll get into the same tent and the same squad; then we'll both volunteer together with special missions. Maybe we'll even get a dangerous night job; then we'll have to use flashlights. And if the flashlights should happen to go out some dark night in enemy territory, I sure don't want to be stranded with someone who doesn't even carry matches!"

IT COULDN'T

The scoffers said it couldn't be done, and the odds were so great, who wouldn't? But I tackled the job that couldn't be done, and what do you know? It couldn't.   *Blue Bell*

SEEMS LOGICAL

He wrecked his car, he lost his job, and yet throughout his life, he took his troubles like a man — he blamed them on his wife!

THAT'S DIFFERENT

While removing finger smudges from the different doors in the house, mother asked, "Joan, are you the little girl who always puts your dirty fingers on the doors?"

"Oh, no, Mother," replied the little girl, "they can't be my fingerprints — I always kick the doors open!"

LOOK PLEASANT

Photographer: Look pleasant, please. As soon as I snap the picture, you can assume your natural expression.

THE DIFFERENCE

A teacher, correcting sixth-grade English themes on the subject of Thanksgiving, came across the following: "Today we have just about the same things to eat. But today we do not have Indians for dinner. We have relatives."

LOTS OF TROUBLE

A ragged hillbilly boy watched a man at a tourist court making use of a comb and brush, a toothbrush, a nail file, and a whisk broom. Finally he asked, "Say, mister, are you always that much trouble to yourself?"

THOMAS EDISON

Thomas Edison was the guest at a dinner. The chairman introduced the inventor with a long account of his inventions. He talked about the marvellous talking machine as the phonograph was then known. Finally he sat down.

Edison arose and began his talk: "I thank the chairman for his kind remarks, but I must make one correction. God invented the talking machine. I only invented the first one that can be shut off."

KNOWN HER LONGER

Two little boys had a favor to ask of their mother. They were afraid she wouldn't grant it. "You ask her," said the older one.

"No, you."

"Go ahead and ask her," the bigger boy repeated.

"No, it would be better if you did it," answered his younger brother. "You've known her longer than I have."

MONEY WAS NO OBJECT

Our psychiatric story of the month concerns the lady who told her doctor that her husband thought himself to be a horse.

"This is a very difficult case," advised the psychiatrist. "He can be cured, but it will take a lot of money."

"Oh, money is no object," declared the wife. "He just won the Kentucky Derby."

PERHAPS

The diner, a chronic complainer, barked at the waiter: "Why is it I never get what I ask for here?"

"Perhaps, sir," the waiter replied, "it's because we are too polite."

EVERYBODY IS DOING IT

When Herbert Hoover was President he gave all his salary back to the government. Now they have us all doing it.

HE HOPES NOT

A Mississippi River steamboat was stopping in the mouth of a tributary stream, because of a dense fog. An inquisitive passenger inquired of the captain the reason for the delay.

"Can't see up the river," was the terse reply.

"But I can see the stars overhead," the passenger replied, sharply.

"Yes," came back the captain, "but unless the boilers bust, we ain't goin' that way!"

ONE WAY TO WIN

An Englishman who was visiting the United States liked it so much that he decided to remain. Some years later he took out his citizenship papers and became a citizen. One day a friend came to visit him from England, and was surprised to find that he had become an American citizen.

"What do you gain by becoming an American?" asked the Britisher.

"Well, for one thing," he replied, "I won the American Revolution!"

THE OLD DAYS

"I can't figure it out," said the small boy, trying to get his father to help him with his arithmetic lesson. "If a carpenter was paid three dollars a day, how much did he earn in four days?"

"No wonder you can't figure it out!" exclaimed the father. "That's not arithmetic — it's ancient history!"

THAT TAUGHT HIM

Five year old Billy ran into the house to tell his mother that four year old Johnny had fallen into the fish pond. She ran out and found Johnny submerged up to his neck and yelling for help. After rescuing him, she asked Billy how it had happened.

"I kept telling him that he was going to fall into the pond if he got too close to the edge."

"But what made him fall in?" demanded his mother.

"I pushed him," was the matter-of-fact reply.

"What?" cried the mother.

"Yes, I pushed him," Billy repeated. "I wanted to show him what would happen if he didn't mind."

EDUCATION

George Gobel says there's a furor raging over education in the United States.

"Those in favor of progressive schools," he continued, "say that in the public schools the kids learn nothing. Those in favor of public schools claim that in progressive schools the kids also learn nothing but they learn it faster."

FUTILE MISSION

A lonely cabin, known to be inhabited, had been sighted in a deep mountain valley almost completely buried by snow drifts.

The rescue squad went into action. The team fought its way down icy crags and cliffs and through heavy snow. Finally they arrived at the mound of snow that covered the cabin. Only the tip of the chimney was visible. Early in the morning they reached the door of the cabin and pried it open.

They found themselves face to face with a gaunt man with a scraggly beard.

"We're from the Red Cross!" they announced triumphantly.

"Wall," drawled the mountain man, scratching his tousled head, "it's been a right tough winter and I don't see how we-uns kin give anything this year."

TO THE HEAD OF THE CLASS

Teacher: "Can you tell me the difference between a stoic and a cynic?"

Boy: "Well, teacher, a stoic is a boid that brings the babies, and a cynic is the place where you wash the dishes."

MOTHER'S PIE

"Willie," said the teacher, "suppose your mother baked an apple pie, and there were seven of you in the family — your parents and five children. What part of the pie would be your portion?"

Without hesitation the boy replied, "One-sixth."

Annoyed at this answer, the teacher persisted, "But, Willie, there are seven of you. Don't you understand fractions?"

"Of course, I understand fractions." Willie retorted. "But I also know my mother. She would say she didn't want any pie!"

OBSERVANT

As a woman was preparing for guests for dinner, her little daughter asked permission to help by putting the silverware around. Permission was gladly granted. Later, when the guests were all seated, the hostess looked up in surprise and exclaimed.

"Why, Mary, you didn't give Mr. Brown a knife and fork!"

Mary replied, "I didn't think he would need any. Daddy says he eats like a horse."

SOUNDS REASONABLE

A lady, after some deep thinking, looked at her husband at the other side of the hearth rug and said, "Listen, darling, I want you to lend me twenty dollars, but only give me ten of them. Then, as I will owe you ten dollars, and you will owe me ten dollars, we can reckon we're square."

NO NEED TO CHECK

A little boy approached Santa in a department store with a long list of requests. He wanted a bicycle, a wagon, a chemical set, a cowboy suit, a set of trains, a football, and roller skates. "That's a pretty long list," Santa said sternly. "I'll have to check in my book and see if you were a good little boy."

"No, never mind checking," the youngster said quickly. "I'll just take the roller skates."

AN UNUSUAL SIGHT

"My dad is an Eagle, a Moose, an Elk, and a Lion," boasted one youngster.

"Yeah?" gasped his wide-eyed companion. "How much does it cost to see him?"

NO FUN

Daddy: "Why don't you want to play with grandpa, Johnny?"

Johnny: "It's no fun, 'cause he's already scalped."

WHO PRINTED IT

A man whose hobby was collecting rare books, became such a bore on the subject that friends decided to play a joke on him. They hired a bit actor and brought him to lunch. When inevitably the subject came up, the actor said he'd had an old German Bible around the house for years, but it smelled so bad he finally gave it away to an aunt in Santa Barbara.

"Who printed it?" the rare-book collector asked.

"I don't know, 'Guten' something," the actor said.

The producer dropped his fork. "Not Gutenberg?"

The actor said he believed that was the name.

The producer jumped up from the table. "Let's go!" he screamed. "We'll hire a plane!"

"Go where?" asked the actor.

"To get the Bible, man! Don't you realize you have one of the first books ever printed? It's worth $300,000!"

The actor stood up excitedly. Then, suddenly, he sat down again. "It can't be worth anything."

"Why not?" asked the producer.

"Because," said the actor, "somebody named Martin Luther wrote all over it."

MIGHT WORK

A small boy stopped at the display of Christmas toys and began screaming and crying. "My mama won't buy me a cap pistol!" he wailed.

"Well, now," said the salesman, "does your mother always buy you what you want whenever you throw one of these fits?"

"No," the boy said. "Sometimes she does and sometimes she doesn't — but it's easy to scream."

TO THE GUARDHOUSE

A rookie stood watching a sergeant as he was writing out a report.

"Well, what do you want?"

"Nothing," replied the rookie.

"Did you bring anything to get it in?" sarcastically asked the sergeant.

"Nope," answered the rookie, "I didn't think you had any left."

WHY NOT?

If one is a tooth and a whole lot are teeth, should not the plural of booth be called beeth? If the masculine pronouns are he, his, and him, imagine the feminine — she — shis, and shim! Then one may be that, and three would be those, yet hat in the plural would never be hose. And if I speak of a foot, and you show me your feet, and I give you a boot, would a pair be called beet?

LOOK OUT

Here are some prevues of coming accidents:

"It's a one-way bridge, but I can get across before that truck comes."

"Guess I'll try the old bus out on this straight stretch; she ought to do 90 anyway."

"Hey, fellows! Watch me come down this pole in a hurry!"

"I can reach that if I stand on a chair."

"Here, let a man show you how to carry that; you don't need two guys for it."

CANDID CADDIE

Player (to caddie): "Well, what do you think of my game?"

Caddie: "I guess it's all right, but I still like golf better."

GOOD EXCUSE

A visitor to a Western hotel asked the clerk about the weather. The clerk had no information, but an Indian standing nearby came up with the answer, "Going rain — much." And so it did.

Awed by the Indian's weather-accuracy, the visitor sought him out the next day for another prediction, and learned it was to be clear and cool. Again the forecast was correct.

The third morning the query was repeated, but this time the Indian smiled and said, "Dunno — radio busted."

IMPOSSIBLE QUESTION

"Nothing that the mind of man can conceive is impossible," declared the professor, with all that finality characteristic of a pedagogue before a class.

"Professor," inquired a student in the back row, "did you ever try to strike a match on a cake of soap?"

THAT EXPLAINS IT

The hillbilly took the pen handed by the hotel clerk and signed the register with an X. After a thoughtful pause, he drew a circle around the X.

"A lot of people sign with an X," said the clerk, "but that's the first time I've ever seen it circled."

"'Tain't nothing odd about it," replied the Ozarkian. "When I'm out for a wild time, I don't use my right name."

TERRIBLE STORY

After years of saving pesos, Jose Gonzales from Mexico City came to Los Angeles to see a professional baseball game.

He found even the standing room was sold out. He pleaded tearfully and touched the heart of a gatekeeper, who permitted him to climb a flagpole to watch the game.

Back home, his comrades gathered round to learn about his experiences in the United States.

"Did they treat you well, Jose?"

"Oh, si!" he declared proudly. "They give me a wonderful seat at the big baseball game, and before the game could start, those Yanquis all stood up and looked up at me and cried out 'Jose, can you see?'"

HARE RAISING TALE

An animal lover hit a hare with his car.

He was distressed. He stopped to watch its suffering and was pondering whether to put it out of its misery when another motorist stopped to offer help.

This was a drug salesman and, going to his sample case, he brought out a bottle and held it under the critter's nose. The rabbit quivered, jumped up, leaped over a shrub and dashed across the field.

"That's wonderful stuff," said the animal lover. "What is it?"

"Oh, just hair restorer."

MY DEAR ALPHONSE!

The prize for courteous repartee was won by William Thackeray. When he was running for office, he happened to meet his opponent one day, who, after chatting amicably, left the great novelist with the remark, "May the best man win!" To which Thackeray replied, "Oh, I hope not."

THAT'S DIFFERENT

Head of the house (in angry tones): "Who told you to put that paper on the wall?"

Decorator: "Your wife, sir."

"Pretty, isn't it?"

ON THE FARM

Once a man out of work had taken a job on a farm. At four o'clock in the morning the newly employed hired man was called to breakfast. A few minutes later the farmer was astonished to see the man walking off down the road.

"Say! Come back and eat breakfast before you go to work." he yelled after him.

"I'm not going to work," the man called back. "I'm going to find a place where I can stay all night."

ON A GUIDED TOUR

Guide: "This is the room where the duke was assassinated."

Tourist: "Indeed! Why, last year you showed us another room."

Guide: "Quite right, sir, but that room is being repainted now."

TAKING HIS TIME

Mother: "Have you said your prayers, Bobby?"

Bobby: "Yes, mother."

Mother: "And did you ask God to make you a good boy?"

Bobby: "Yes, mother — but not yet."

FORCED ON HIM

A speaker's appearance on a program may be much like the experience of a man who had just been married. He had been a bit nervous throughout the nuptial ceremonies, and when it came time for the wedding dinner, he was congratulating himself that the worst was over. He soon discovered his mistake when he was unexpectedly called on for a speech. The embarrassed young man rose with some confusion, looked about at the guests, and, making a helpless gesture toward his bride, stammered, "This — er — thing has been forced on me."

ABNORMAL

After the first week of school, officials required teachers to fill out forms about their new classes. One question was: "Have you any abnormal children in your class?"

"Yes," wrote the teacher. And in the blank space for explanation, she wrote: "'Two of them have good manners."

AND THEN

The retiring usher was instructing his youthful successor in the details of his office. "And remember, my boy, that we have nothing but good, kind Christians in this church — until you try to put someone else in their pew."

WATCH THE LINE

There is a line on the ocean where you lose a day when you cross it.

There is a line on most highways where you can do even better.

SPEECHLESS SPEAKER

Many a speaker could find reason for pause in the remarks by a sixth grade pupil who was asked to stand up and speak before his English class.

"I ain't got nothing to say," he admitted, "but I will say it anyhow."

Conversely, there are many businessmen who have very important things to say, but just don't get around to saying them.

Like telling their good customers "thank you."

COULD BE

Foolish questions are said to deserve answers in kind, as witness the story about the nosey tourist who couldn't ask enough questions.

"Tell me," he demanded of his cowboy guide, "what makes these western plains so flat?"

"Reckon," drawled the cowhand, "it's 'cause the sun sets on 'em every night."

CYNIC!

Love is like an onion, you taste with delight, and when it's gone you wonder whatever made you bite!

DIPLOMATIC

Judge O'Flaherty: "Haven't you been before me before?"

Prisoner: "No, your honor. I never saw but one face that looked like yours and that was a photograph of an Irish King."

Judge O'Flaherty: "Discharged. Call the next case."

HE HAD A REASON

Wife: "I simply can't understand, John, why you always sit on the piano stool whenever we have company. Everyone knows that you can't play a note."

Husband: "I know it dear. And, as long as I'm sitting there, neither can anybody else."

HARD TO BELIEVE

It's hard to believe that just 100 years ago people were crossing this country in wagon trains. Today they're all home watching "Wagon Train" on TV.

A DEPENDABLE NUISANCE

"Have you any alarm clocks?" inquired the customer. "What I want is one that will arouse father without waking the whole family."

"I don't know of any such alarm clock," said the man behind the counter. "We keep just the ordinary kind that will wake the whole family without disturbing father."

BACK TO REST UP

My vacation is over, my postcarding through; the snap-shotting's finished — the suntanning, too. That sweet summer romance is a thing of the past, and I — I'm back at the office, to rest up at last!

CLEAN CUP

Three men decided to stop at a downtown restaurant for a pot of tea. The waiter appeared with pad and pencil.

"I want a cup of weak tea," ordered one.

"I'd like tea, too," said the second, "but strong."

"Tea for me, too," ordered the third man; "medium strong, but be sure the cup is absolutely clean."

In a short time the waiter returned with the order. "Which one," he asked, "gets the clean cup?"

CORRECT

Teacher: "Johnny, where is Madagascar?"
Johnny, stalling: "Where do you think it is?"
Teacher: "I don't think, I know."
Johnny: "I don't think I know, either."

ERRORS IN THE NEWS

Fifty guests assembled at the Domestic Forum, and thirty have been married to the same man for more than twenty years.

Leo Drau is at the Memorial Hospital. He is suffering from head injuries and shock caused by coming into contact with a live wife.

It is with real regret that we learn of Mr. Shaigh's recovery from an automobile accident.

At the Ladies Aid rummage sale many interesting articles were sold. Every member brought something she no longer needed. Many members brought their husbands.

FAIR DEAL

A young man wrote to a business firm, ordering a razor: "Dear Sirs: Please find enclosed fifty cents for one of your razors as advertised. P.S. I forgot to enclose the fifty cents, but no doubt a firm of your high standing will send the razor anyway."

The firm addressed thus replied: "Dear Sir: Your most valued order received the other day and we are sending the razor as per request, and hope it will prove satisfactory. P.S. We forgot to enclose the razor, but no doubt a man with your cheek will have no need of it."

BENJAMIN FRANKLIN

Asked to write a brief essay on the life of Benjamin Franklin, one little girl wrote this paragraph:

"He was born in Boston, traveled to Philadelphia, met a lady on the street, she laughed at him, he married her, and discovered electricity."

EMOTION

There was a little dachshund once so long he had no notion how long it took to notify his tail of his emotion. And thus it was that while his eyes were filled with woe and sadness, his little tail kept wagging on because of previous gladness.

WHAT YOU'RE DOING NOW

It's not what you'd do with a million, if riches should be your lot, but what you're doing now with the buck and a half you've got.

BUSY

"I putter, I worry, I push and shove, hunting little mole-hills to make mountains of."

BE CAREFUL

To avoid that "run down feeling," here's advice you cannot beat: Be very, very careful when crossing a busy street.

LANGUAGE

How involved a statement may become is shown by the following excerpt said to be from a speech by Federal Judge Roy W. Harper.

"If one of you had an orange which you wanted to give to your neighbor, you would do so by probably saying, 'I give you this orange.' But the people with whom I deal primarily — lawyers — if they were giving you the orange, would probably say, 'I give you all and singularly my estate and interest, right, title, and claim, and advantage of and in this orange with all its rind, skin, juice, pulp, and pips, and all rights and advantages therein, with full power to bite, suck, or otherwise eat the same or give the same away with or without its rind, skin, juice, pulp, and pips, anything heretofore or hereinafter or in any deed or deeds, instrument or instruments of whatever kind or nature to the contrary in anywise nowithstanding.' "

DAD'S PREPARED

A college boy sent a telegram home saying, "Mom! Have failed all subjects. Prepare Dad."

The reply came the next day, "Dad prepared — prepare yourself."

FOND OF HIM

Visitor: "I suppose the new baby is fond of you?"
Father: "Fond of me! Why, he sleeps all day when I'm not at home and stays up all night to enjoy my company."

KEEP OUR HIGHWAYS BEAUTIFUL

This year there will be a highway beautification program of sorts. New campaign posters will cover the tattered old ones.   *Wichita (Kan.) Eagle*

A GOOD ONE, TOO

"Well, madam," said the psychiatrist, "I think we've got your kleptomania under control now."
The woman smiled and got up to leave.
"However," warned the doctor, "if you feel yourself having a relapse, pick me up one of those little transistor radios, will you?"

THIS BURNED HIM

I always liked the one about the lawyer who when reading the dear departed's will came to this line, "And to my brother-in-law George, who was always telling me that health is more important than wealth, I leave my sun lamp!"

NO LONG SPEECH

Senator Hugh Scott tells of the sick Indian who was visited in the hospital by a fellow brave. Asked how he felt, the

Indian answered, "Ugh." As to the food, he gave the same answer.

"And how you like nurse?" asked the visitor.

"Ugh, ugh, ugh," the sick Indian replied.

"I ask simple question," said the first brave. "Don't make long speech."

COMPLETE EXPERIENCE

A secretary was applying for a new job. Under office experience on the application blank she wrote: "I'm familiar with all important phases of office procedure, including bowling, crossword puzzles, coffee breaks, personal letter writing and collection taking."

PRETTY AWFUL JOKE

Doctor: "How's the patient who swallowed the spoon?"
Nurse: "He can hardly stir!"

IMPOSSIBLE

Father, looking over report card, to small son: "One thing in your favor — with these grades, you couldn't possibly be cheating."

SEEMS LOGICAL

All Summer Paul watched Eddie give demonstrations on how to putt. Ed, who sometimes wears glasses, seldom missed a putt, even from the edge of the green. Finally, at the end of the Summer, Paul asked how he holed out so accurately.

"Well," said Ed, "these glasses of mine are bifocals. When I line up a putt, I look through the edges of the two lenses so I see two balls, one small and one big, and two holes, one small and one big. Then it's simple. I just knock the small ball in the big hole."

PATIENCE

On a rural gas station: Buzz twice for night service. Then keep your shirt on while I get my pants on.

IF

Two youngsters were standing on the corner waiting for the lights to change. Cars were driving through lights and stop signs, double parking, and weaving in an out of traffic lanes. Said one child to the other with a sigh, "What do you want to be if you grow up?"

THAT EXPLAINS IT

A youngster walked into a bank to open an account with $25.
The teller smiled and asked him how he had accumulated so much money.
"Selling magazine subscriptions," said the boy.
"You've done very well. Lots of people must have bought them."
"Nope," answered the boy proudly, "Only one family — their dog bit me."

SPECIAL

Small boy to father: "There's a special P.T.A. meeting tonight — just you, my teacher, and the principal."

DOESN'T TAKE LONG

A little city boy spent a night on the farm for the first time. Next morning, much earlier than he was accustomed to rise, he was awakened by the activity on the farm around him. Coming downstairs, he remarked: "You know something: it doesn't take long to stay here all night, does it?"

IS THAT CLEAR

The speaker beginning his talk at a club meeting advised: "My job, as I understand it, is to talk to you. Your's as I understand it, is to listen. If you finish before I do, just hold up your hand."

REMEMBER

Chairman of the board to the other officers: "Of course, it's only a suggestion, gentlemen, but let's not forget who's making it."

THAT'S DIFFERENT

The responsibilities of the Vice President of the United States have grown in recent years but most Americans still seem to regard the Vice President much the same as a fireman did when Calvin Coolidge held that office.

Coolidge was living at the Willard Hotel in Washington when a fire broke out late at night and the guests were obliged to leave their rooms for the street. When the fire was under control, Coolidge started to reenter the hotel and return to bed but was halted by a fireman.

"But I'm the Vice President," Coolidge protested.

"All right, you can go in," the fireman said, stepping aside, then asking suspiciously: "Vice President of what?"

"I'm the Vice President of the United States," Coolidge replied.

"I'm sorry," the fireman said, "but you can't enter. I thought you were the vice president of this hotel."

CHAPTER VII

USEFUL MATERIAL FOR MANY OCCASIONS

CONFIDENCE

You can't argue with confidence. A personnel man reports that he was more than a little impressed by one young man.

To the question, why did you leave your previous job? (temporary sorter at the postoffice), he replied, "Did all the work!"

And to the question, "Why did you leave the Armed Forces?" he answered: "Won the War."

DO IT NOW

The clock of life is wound but once, and no man has the power to tell us when the hands will stop, at late or early hour. Now is the only time you own; live, love, toil with a will; place no faith in tomorrow for the clock may then be still.

PUNCTUALITY

A friend of ours says his secretary told him: "I'm not really late, boss, I just took my coffee break before coming in."

HELP!

Backward, turn backward,
O time in thy flight,
I've just got a wise crack
I needed last night.

TOO OFTEN

In the world's great field of battle,
In the bivouacs of life,
You will find the Christian soldier
Represented by his wife.

GOOD ADVICE

Stop and let the trains go by — it hardly takes a minute. Your car starts out again intact, and — better still — you're in it!   *Sunshine Magazine*

GREATNESS

Great minds discuss ideas, average minds discuss events, small minds discuss people.

NOT WHAT IT USED TO WAS!

I remember, I remember, ere my childhood flitted by, it was cold then in December, and was warmer in July. In the winter there were freezings, in the summer there were thaws; but the weather isn't now at all like it used to was!

CHILDREN

Children are a comfort in our old age, it is true; and very often children help us reach it faster, too.

STRONG NATIONS

I am aware of and thank God for statistics which tell us that almost one hundred million people in America believe in

God and have some kind of religious faith. But, what of the other seventy million Americans who live on the by-products of the investment in faith by other generations? What about those who name the name of Christ, but do not live the life of Christ? "O Israel," Hosea said in a day of perpetual crises, "O Israel, thou hast destroyed thyself." And it was true. *It was true.* Moral suicide can happen in America. The seeds of self-destruction may very well be sown in this "land of the free and the home of the brave."

I was rereading some of the writings of one of the greatest historians of our time which reminded me of the cycles through which the nations of the world have gone. Nations become strong because they are captive to ideals. Vitality springs from the people and this leads to power, and power to world prestige. Power is always accompanied by wealth. The by-product of wealth is often luxury and softness which lead to the deterioration of moral fiber and stature, plus the compromise of the ideals which once made a nation great. When softness and spiritual decadence set in, then moral suicide takes place. What enemies from without could not accomplish, disintegration from within assures. Thus the mills of God and history grind slowly, but exceedingly fine. Call the roll of the nations of the world: Babylonia, Greece, Rome and on down through the present day. The epitaph is always the same: "thou hast destroyed thyself." This is the testimony, not of a little group of people precious to the heart of God, but the inexorable testimony of history.

I have said from this pulpit time and time again that it is not beyond the realm of possibility that Russia and world-wide Communism can match us in every piece of military equipment and in every scientific achievement. This is *possible.* But, there is one thing that Russia cannot match us in if we possess it — that is spiritual commitment to the One True God and the moral grandeur that stems from faith in His Son. This faith produces courage which comes from a man who, having bowed at the Cross and risen up clean, knows that if he can face God, he can face any demonic power on earth or in hell. If we do not have faith and courage to offer to our generation in its perpetual crises, what under God do we have to offer?

From a sermon by Dr. Robert J. Lamont

INTERESTING DEFINITIONS

Auction — A place where you are liable to get something for nodding.

Blush — Rainbow of modesty.

Brat — A child who acts like yours but belongs to a neighbor.

Budget — A mathematical confirmation of your suspicion.

Committee — A group of persons appointed to complicate and confuse simple matters.

Compliment — A remark that need not be true to be gratefully received.

Dieting — The penalty for exceeding the feed limit.

Diplomat — A person who tries to solve the problems caused by other diplomats.

Education — Learning a lot about how little you know.
Franklin P. Jones

Elephant — Eight thousand pounds of liver with legs. (School boy's definition)

Enough — More than you have.

Equality — A form of self-deception which makes the incompetent satisfied with themselves.

Gentleman — A man who acts unselfishly to attain selfish objectives.

Headwaiter — A tyrant without ears or eyes dressed in a tuxedo.

Highbrow — A lowbrow who is clever enough to conceal it.

Honesty — An honest man is one who has traveled abroad and hasn't the slightest idea of how to save the world.

Husband — A curious creature who buys his football tickets in June and his wife's Christmas present on December 24th.

Laughter — The annoying sound the other person makes when you get what you didn't have coming.

Memory — The thing that suddenly tells a man his wife's birthday was yesterday.

Middle age — The period when you feel ten years older and try to act ten years younger than you really are.

Opinion — A definite conclusion reached after examining one's preconceived ideas.   *Wall Street Journal*

Optimist — A person who takes a big basket when he goes shopping with three dollars.

Poise — The ability to be ill at ease naturally.

Practical joker — A man who has a large jocular vein.

Reception — A big party without chairs.

Scholar — A person with too much brains to be able to earn a large salary.

Show-off — A person who is shown-up in a show-down.

Silence — The hardest argument to refute.

Smile — The whisper of a laugh.

Spring — The season when boys begin to feel gallant, and galls buoyant.

Television hero — One who sits through the program.

Tipping — What you give to have your luncheon served before dinner.

Tourist — A person who travels 1,000 miles to get a picture of himself standing by his car.

Waiter — A person who can't hear or see and who goes around with his palms open.

Washington — The only city where people are paid to keep the rest of us worried.

THIS MEANS TROUBLE

There are two kinds of business: yours and the other person's. Many people can't tell them apart.

THE CROSS

The trouble with us is that we like to be near enough to bask in Christ's glory, but not near enough to help carry the cross.

MONEY

If a man's after money, he's money-mad.
If he keeps it, he's a capitalist.
If he spends it, he's a playboy.
If he doesn't get it, he's a ne'er-do-well.

If he doesn't try to get it, he lacks ambition.
If he gets it without working for it, he's a parasite —
And if he accumulates it after years of toil,
    people call him a fool who never got anything out of life.

UNIVERSITY PRESIDENT

I am simply a university president. And any academician will tell you that that is the lowest form of academic life. You've heard several times, of course, that a dean is a man not quite clever enough to be a professor, but much too clever to be a president.

    F. Cyril James, Vice-Chancellor, McGill University

A SUGGESTION

"I see that at your Church Convention," said an old farmer to the preacher, "you discussed the subject: 'How to Get People to Attend Church.' I have never heard a single address at a farmers' convention on how to get the cattle to come to eat. We spend our time discussing the best kind of feed."   *National Health Federation Bulletin*

WHO CAN SPEAK FOR AMERICA?

The hope of the United States in the present and in the future is the same that it has always been: it is the hope and confidence that out of unknown homes will come men who will constitute themselves the masters of industry and of politics. The average hopefulness, the average welfare, the average enterprise, the average initiative of the United States are the only things that make it rich. We are not rich because a few gentlemen direct our industry; we are rich because of our own intelligence and our own industry.

America does not consist of men who get their names into the newspapers; America does not consist politically of the men who set themselves up to be political leaders; she does not consist of the men who do most of her talking — they are important only so far as they speak for the great voiceless multitude of men who constitute the body and the saving force of the nation.

Nobody who cannot speak the common thought, who does not move by the common impulse, is the man to speak for America, or for any of her future purposes. Only he is fit to speak who knows the thoughts of the great body of citizens, the men who go about their business every day, the men who toil from morning to night, the men who go home tired in the evenings, the men who are carrying on the things of which we are so proud.   *Woodrow Wilson*

PRAYER

The spectacle of a nation praying is more awe-inspiring than the explosion of an atomic bomb. The force of prayer is greater than any possible combination of man-controlled powers because prayer is man's greatest means of tapping the resources of God.   *J. Edgar Hoover*

INDUSTRY AND GENIUS

After a great deal of experience and observation, I have become convinced that industry is a better horse to ride than genius. It may never carry any man as far as genius has carried individuals, but industry — patient, steady, intelligent industry — will carry thousands into comfort, and even celebrity; and this it does with absolute certainty.
                    Walter Lippmann

WHAT MAKES MAN

It is not what men eat but what they digest that makes them strong; not what we gain, but what we save that makes us rich; not what we read, but what we remember that makes us learn; and not what we preach, but what we practice that makes us Christians.   *Francis Bacon*

FREE SPEECH

We live in a free country where a man can say what he thinks if he isn't afraid of his wife, his neighbors, his boss, his customers or the government.

A SNEEZE

I sneezed a sneeze into the air,
It fell to earth I know not where;
But hard and cold were the looks of those
In whose vicinity I snoze.

ON PLYMOUTH ROCK

This inscription appears on Plymouth Rock Monument in Massachusetts: "This monument marks the first burying ground in Plymouth of the passengers of the 'Mayflower.' Here, under cover of darkness, the fast dwindling company laid their dead, leveling the earth above them lest the Indians should learn how many were the graves. History records no nobler venture for faith and freedom than of this Pilgrim band. In weariness and painfulness, in watching often in hunger and cold, they laid the foundation of a state wherein every man through countless ages should have liberty to worship God in his own way. May their example inspire thee to do thy part in perpetuating and spreading the lofty ideals of our republic throughout the world."

THE FAMOUS PHRASE

If 100 persons are asked who first said, "of the people, by the people, for the people," probably 99 out of the 100 will reply, "Lincoln"; and, in all probability, the hundredth will add, "in his Gettysburg address."

The famous phrase, familiar to millions of school children and their elders, actually is 578 years old, and once appeared in the Bible! In John Wycliffe's introduction to his translation of the Bible, published in England in 1382, these words occurred: "This Bible is for the Government of the People, by the People, and for the People."

ANCESTRY

They talk about their Pilgrim blood,
   Their birthright high and holy!
A mountain-stream that ends in mud
   Methinks is melancholy.   *J. R. Lowell*

BREVITY

Since brevity is the soul of wit,
And tediousness the limbs and outward flourishes,
I will be brief.   *Shakespeare*

MANKIND'S CONCERN

In Faith and Hope the world will disagree,
But all mankind's concern is Charity.
                              Alexander Pope

CONSCIENCE

Conscience is a God to all mortals.   *Menander*
Conscience is the voice of the soul.   *Jean J. Rousseau*
My conscience hath a thousand several tongues.
                                    Shakespeare
Conscience does make cowards of us all.   *Shakespeare*

BRAVERY

Certainly no one who thinks pain the greatest evil can be
brave; nor thinking pleasure the greatest good, temperate.
                                        Cicero
The brave man is not he who feels no fear,
For that were stupid and irrational;
But he, whose noble soul its fear subdues,
And bravely dares the danger nature shrinks from.
                              Joanna Baillie

CYNIC

What is a cynic? A man who knows the price of everything, and the value of nothing.   *Oscar Wilde*

DAYS OF THE WEEK

Monday's child is fair of face,
Tuesday's child is full of grace,
Wednesday's child is full of woe,
Thursday's child has far to go,
Friday's child is loving and giving,
Saturday's child works hard for its living,
And a child that's born on the Sabbath day
Is fair and wise and good and gay.   *Anonymous*

ELOQUENCE

Talking and eloquence are not the same: to speak and to speak well, are two things. A fool may talk, but a wise man speaks.   *Ben Jonson*

Inebriated with the exuberance of his own verbosity.
                    Benjamin Disraeli

The finest eloquence is that which gets things done.
                    David Lloyd George

It is the heart which renders men eloquent: Pectus est quod disertos facit.   *Quintilian*

FAITH

There are no tricks in plain and simple faith.
                    Shakespeare

For what is faith, unless it is to believe what you do not see?   *St. Augustine*

You can do very little with faith, but you can do nothing without it.   *Samuel Butler*

I have fought a good fight, I have finished my course, I

have kept the faith.   *Second Timothy, 4,7*
    Faith without works is dead.   *James, 2,20*

FAME

Fame is the spur that the clear spirit doth raise
(That last infirmity of noble mind)
To scorn delights, and live laborious days.
                                        John Milton

What, after all, is undying fame? Complete vanity.
                                        Marcus Aurelius

Fame's but a hollow echo.   *Sir Walter Raleigh*

Sir, if they should cease to talk of me, I must starve.
                                        Dr. Samuel Johnson

The boast of heraldry, the pomp of pow'r,
    And all that beauty, all that wealth e'er gave,
Awaits alike th' inevitable hour,
    The paths of glory lead but to the grave.
                                        Thomas Gray

MAN

Created half to rise, and half to fall;
Great lord of all things, yet a prey to all;
Sole judge of truth, in endless error hurl'd;
The glory, jest, and riddle of the world.
                                        Alexander Pope

What a piece of work is man! how noble in reason! how
infinite in faculty! in form and moving how express and
admirable! in action how like an angel! in apprehension how
like a god! the beauty of the world! the paragon of animals!
And yet, to me, what is this quintessence of dust?
                                        Shakespeare

EXPLAIN THIS

A friend recently gave this puzzling statement of his account at the bank:

Deposited	$50	in the bank,	then
Drew out	$20	leaving	$30
Drew out	15	leaving	15
Drew out	9	leaving	6
Drew out	6	leaving	0
Total	$50	Total	$51

EDUCATION

Perhaps the most valuable result of all education is the ability to make yourself do the things you have to do when they ought to be done, whether you like it or not. It is the first lesson that ought to be learned; and however early a man's training begins, it is probably the last lesson he learns thoroughly.   *Thomas Henry Huxley*

SPELLING

They spell it Vinci and pronounce it Vincy; foreigners always spell better than they pronounce.   *Mark Twain*

GREATNESS

Greatness is a spiritual condition worthy to excite love, interest, and admiration; and the outward proof of possessing greatness is, that we excite love, interest, and admiration.
Matthew Arnold

It is the habit of the mob to snarl at great men, much as little dogs bark at strangers.   *Seneca*

LIFE

Life is a sheet of paper white
Whereon each one of us may write
His word or two, and then comes night.
J. R. Lowell

Life is mostly froth and bubble;
　Two things stand like stone:
Kindness in another's trouble,
　　Courage in your own.　　*Adam Lindsay Gordon*

Life's but a walking shadow; a poor player
That struts and frets his hour upon the stage,
And then is heard no more.　　*Shakespeare*

No man is an island, entire of itself; every man is a piece
of the continent . . .; any man's death diminishes me, because
I am involved in mankind; and therefore never send to
know for whom the bell tolls; it tolls for thee.　　*Donne*

THE THREE BONES

An Irish father was seeing his son off on the steamship to
a new land where the lad was going with the intention of
seeking his fortune in a new way of life.

"Now, Michael, my boy," said the elderly man, as they
parted, "remember the three bones, and ye'll always get along
all right."

A stranger standing nearby overheard the remark, and
when the ship had gone, he inquired of the old gentleman
what three bones he had referred to in his parting advice to
his son.

"Sure, now," responded the old Irishman, "and wouldn't
it be the wishbone and the jawbone and the backbone? It's
the wishbone that keeps you going after things, and it's the
jawbone that helps you find out how to go after them if you
are not too proud to ask a question when there's something
you don't know, and it's the backbone that keeps you at it
till you get there!"　　*Sunshine Magazine*

ECONOMIST HINDSIGHT

Today's prices prove that the best time to buy anything is
a year ago.　　*Avon (N. Y.) Gazette and Independent*

WHAT IS INVENTION?

Invention, strictly speaking, is little more than a new combination of those images which have been previously gathered and deposited in the memory. Nothing can be made of nothing; he who has laid up no material can produce no combinations.   *Sir Joshua Reynolds*

THE PURPOSE OF BUSINESS

No enterprise can exist for itself alone. It ministers to some great need, it performs some great service, not for itself, but for others; or failing therein, it ceases to be profitable and ceases to exist.   *Calvin Coolidge*

GREAT PLANS

It is a hard rule of life, and I believe a healthy one, that no great plan is ever carried out without meeting and overcoming endless obstacles that come up to try the skill of man's hand, the quality of his courage and the endurance of his faith.   *Donald Douglas*

THE GREATEST ASSET

The greatest asset of any nation is the spirit of its people, and the greatest danger that can menace any nation is the breakdown of that spirit — the will to win and the courage to work.   *George B. Cortelyou*

THE WISE MAN

That which the fool does in the end the wise man does in the beginning.   *R. C. Trench*

TRY THIS ONE

Husband to wife: "How do you expect me to remember your birthday when you never look any older?"

THE FAITH OF OUR FATHERS

The hope of the world lies in a return to the faith of our fathers, and a universal acceptance of the Supreme Being who guides our destiny.   *John Edgar Hoover*

BRUSH YOUR BRAIN

You should not only brush your teeth each day, but you should also brush your brain to get the cobwebs out.
          George W. Crane

HOPE

I know my dreams won't all come true — I'm not that big a dope. But there's no statute on the books that says I don't dare hope!

FATHER'S DAY

Here's to Dad on Father's Day — the old man is a hunny! We hope and pray he likes those gifts, for they're going to cost him munny!

HE LISTENED

His thoughts were slow, his words were few, and never formed to glisten, but he was joy to all his friends — you should have heard him listen!

HOW TO TELL

When cold in the air makes stars very bright, when none of the youngsters can wait for the night; and you think of a wrong that you want to make right — that's Christmas! Yes, sir, that's Christmas!

GIVING THANKS

For what shall a man give thanks? For the simple blessings of the day. For the laughter of a child. For grass and trees and water and sunshine; the soft tumult of the leaves, and the friendly bark of a dog. For neighbors and friends and strangers, who pause to bestow acts of kindness. For the calm of the night, and a star-filled sky to light the dark way. For warm firesides and still shadows. For the smile of the stranger to remind us to smile again. For the physician's soothing hand, the scientist's impenetrable mysteries; for all who mobilize for human need and happiness. For all these, and the countless good, let us give thanks.

Adapted from Gabriel Heatter

THE OYSTER AND THE EAGLE

When God made the oyster, He guaranteed him absolute economic and social security. He built the oyster a house, a shell to protect him from his enemies. When hungry, the oyster simply opens up his shell and the food rushes in. But when God made the eagle, He said, "The blue sky is the limit. Go build your own house." And the eagle went out and built his house on the highest mountain crag, where storms threaten him every day. For food, he flies through miles of rain and snow and wind. The eagle, and not the oyster, is the emblem of America.

PEACE ON EARTH

The Swedish people have an interesting way of decorating their Christmas trees. Many families in that country attach their national flag to the very top of the tree, and on the other branches of the evergreen they place small flags of many other nations of the earth as a symbol of the true Christmas message of "Peace on earth, good will to men."

Sunshine Magazine

THE DOUBTER

About a century and a half ago, when the first American steamship, Robert Fulton's *Clermont,* was scheduled to make its trial run on the Hudson River, a crowd gathered to watch the spectacle. One of the spectators was a pessimistic old farmer, who predicted gloomily, "They'll never start her!"

But the steamboat did start. Its speed increased. Faster and faster it went, belching black, billowing smoke from its funnel; and the crowd on the river banks went wild with enthusiasm.

But the old farmer turned away, shaking his head, hardly able to believe what he saw. "They'll never stop her!" he declared.

PRESIDENTS OF THE UNITED STATES

Seven Presidents of the United States — Lincoln, Jefferson, Jackson, Fillmore, Buchanan, Garfield, and Arthur — were born in log cabins. Eight Presidents never went to college; 23 were lawyers by profession. Tyler was the first chief executive to be photographed, Taft the first one to play golf, and McKinley the first to have an auto.

Sunshine Magazine

HARD TO TELL

There's so much good in the worst of us, and so much bad in the best of us, that it's hard to tell which one of us ought to reform the rest of us.

FALLOUT SHELTERS

We have seen lists of things recommended to be taken into a fallout shelter. These lists recommended such things as radio, TV, food, tranquilizers, and . . . a stock of liquor. So far, on any of these lists, there has been no mention of the Bible.

We have seen "cut away" illustrations of fallout shelters, exposing for all to see, people inside, relaxing in comfort — reading or watching TV — blissfully unaware, or oblivious to, the pitter-patter of death on the roof without. These interior views have shown cans of goods, tranquilizer pills within reach, "makings" for martinis.

We have not seen in any of these views thus exposed, the Bible opened to the Twenty-third Psalm. Sort of made us wonder.   *The Lake Mills (Wis.) Leader*

INDEX

INDEX (Continued)